BURN YOUR BED

The surprising story behind the
500th New Testament translation

Edward Speyers

Foreword by
Laura Mae Gardner

prove God strong.

Yes, buy the book! It has lots of everything in it. I was moved by Ed's father leaving the family with "his" half of everything, including half of the silverware, and Ed cheering his mother on the following Christmas with lights strung up next to their farmhouse, which his father never approved. His mother always called it "The Christmas of 1974." But you may like other parts—how Canadian Ed and American Linda met, the letter from heaven, or the Wycliffe-designated 500th translation which providentially turned out to be the one finished in Suriname, or the recruitment results through the years after the Bible translation.

—Thea Van Halsema
Former Professor of Social Work/Dean of Students Reformed Bible College

During all my years at Wycliffe Bible Translators, I've witnessed tremendous milestones in bringing Scripture to people in the languages they know and understand best. One of the most memorable was the publication of the 500th New Testament translation, in Suriname Javanese, brought about in large part through the steadfast work and ministry of colleagues Ed and Linda Speyers. Ed's new book, Burn Your Bed, is a wonderful reflection on the lifelong, generational faithfulness of God and a triumphal retelling of the development of this milestone translation.

—Bob Creson
President/CEO Wycliffe Bible Translators USA

This story is a must read! Not only is it captivating, but the words of forgiveness and healing are like a soothing balm for hurting hearts. Each chapter will encourage your faith and strengthen you, helping you to see God's steadfast love and faithfulness in your own story.

—Nancy Thomas, MSN, RN
Associate Professor of Nursing, Evening Coordinator
Cleveland State Community College

Ed Speyers offers a refreshingly candid account of the challenges and joys of an immigrant growing up in Canada who yielded himself to God and to joining His mission. This book shows us that, no matter who we are, it's not our limitations that define us. God's power is the difference maker in crafting a remarkable life story.

—Roy Eyre
President Wycliffe Bible Translators of Canada

Have you ever wondered how prayer works in the life of a believer, in discerning what work we are to do in God's world, in overcoming setbacks or self-doubt? Ed's new book, Burn Your Bed, is a great resource for answering such questions.

—Marc Baer, Professor of History, Hope College and author of *Mere Believers*

Hemingway said, "Every life, well told, is a novel." Here's a life that definitely should be told. And, better, it's not a novel, but the real stuff. And, though there's so much life packed in, it's told so succinctly that the suggestion of what's left out is just as intriguing.

It's not just the life of Ed and Linda Speyers, rather it's the life of God in the life of Ed and Linda Speyers. As such, how could it not be full of interest, full of lessons, full of overcoming, full of wonder, and full of joy? Bravo, Ed and Linda!

—Hyatt Moore
Artist, (former president of Wycliffe Bible Translators, USA)

You will both rejoice and be challenged by <u>Burn Your Bed</u>. As you read you will clearly see all of the ways God has 'gone before' Ed and Linda in their lives and ministry. Every page is a reminder that the Speyers have been on a journey with God in His Mission of reconciling all nations to Himself.

Parents will want to follow the example of Ed's mother of faithful prayers, love, and encouragement. Young people will be challenged as they are reminded that trusting God fully leads to opportunities beyond imagination. I believe every reader will also rejoice in knowing that the Suriname Javanese people have access to God's message of love in their heart language.

—Steve Sheldon
Language Program Advisor/Partner Relations Advisor for Wycliffe USA

As I finished reading through the chapters I said, "Wow, there it is again!" Ed has effectively portrayed the beautiful results when a normal young man makes the outrageous decision to follow God's purpose for his life no matter what, no matter where, and backs it up with action.

The story is terrific, but not so much because of what it reveals about Ed. I've known Ed for over 30 years and the book doesn't really touch on his giftedness and why he is so loved by so many. The story is most remarkable in what it reveals about his loving, faithful, powerful, and eternal Father.

—Jerry Long
Founder and President of Kingdom Come Training
Former Wycliffe International Training Consultant

Contents

Foreword

I have known Ed and Linda Speyers for a number of years, connecting with them in meaningful ways from time to time. My husband and I are part of the same mission organization, so this book rings true and loudly to us. Some descriptive words are: starkly personal, powerful, vulnerable and transparent, enchanting, and motivational.

Ed is telling his own story; he doesn't intend it to be a textbook for missions, yet that's what it is. Some of the lessons that stand out here are:

- Learn to work hard, regardless of how humble the task before him is;
- An amazing conversion story, centered around music;
- Constantly seeking God's will;
- The humility necessary when moving into another culture—in just two minutes he was reduced to the level of a child in that language and culture;
- There is a price to pay for living overseas—and both sides of the family pays that price;
- Take advantage of every opportunity to engage in learning activities;
- Living without anything, learning what it is that a missionary does;
- Leading a principled life, beginning with a posture toward debt, family chores, etc.;
- Illustrating how to carry on a task without waiting for ideal circumstances;
- When asked to move into a different role, he did so—and found it awakened new gifts;
- Moving on to the next task;
- Living with joy and delight;
- Unlearning some lessons of his childhood with regard to how a godly father and husband behaves toward family members—and learning new ones toward his own family.

Ed's story is a blessing and an encouragement. He sees himself as an average man; I see him as a giant. After reading this book, you'll see him that way too.

—Laura Mae Gardner, D.Min.
Former International Vice President for Personnel SIL and Wycliffe
Author of *Healthy, Resilient, and Effective in Cross-Cultural Ministry*

Acknowledgements

It's a privilege to acknowledge the individuals who have made this book possible. My greatest ally and confidant is undoubtedly my wife, Linda. Her loving and gentle manner have been my mainstay since we married in 1977. Thank you honey, for always building me up with your positive remarks.

Our sons David and Mark, were born in Suriname and like so many MKs (missionary kids), would play a huge role in the daunting task that lay before us, starting in 1979. As children, you opened doors that we couldn't, doors to the language and culture of the Suriname Javanese. We love you both. You're now married to lovely women yourselves. The word on the street is that it's still an arguable point if you qualify for the office of the President of the United States, having been born overseas. We'll see.

My mother, Tryntye Speyers-Pronk, was a constant encouragement and inspiration to me growing up, and well into my adult years. We miss Mom but her love continues and inspires.

I subjected many friends to listen to a chapter or two while I was still in the early writing stages. In the end, they continually encouraged me to publish the book you're now holding. My thanks goes out to you for your patience and helpful suggestions.

Jerry Long taught me the value and technique of telling a story in three minutes and moving on to the next. Many of the chapters are based on that principle, although they have been fleshed out considerably for the reader's sake. I treasure your friendship, Jerry.

Dedication

This book is dedicated to our granddaughters, Emily and Jessica and any other grandchildren that the Lord brings along the way.

A note from the author

It was 1980, and I was sitting on Frits Mastenbroek's balcony overlooking the Suriname River, a tropical breeze wafting across our faces. We drank strong Douwe Egberts coffee. Dolphins played in the distance, frolicking in the muddy waters. Frits, a school teacher turned Bible educator, was from the Netherlands and had made Suriname his home many years before our arrival. I counted it a privilege to be in his company and made it a regular habit to visit this wise man who was well into his 70s. He said, "Ed, you've come to Suriname to tackle a difficult work and I applaud you for it. There are three small pieces of advice that I want to give you. First, I want you to listen. Listen to what people in this country are saying. Listen before you offer your opinion or advice. If you open your mouth too soon, you will miss what living in this country means. Second, I want you to listen. Listen carefully to your leaders because you are a neophyte to Suriname. You are brand new to this culture. You have come with idealism, eagerness, and many ideas ready to tackle the job of Bible translation, but if you fail to listen, all of that will be meaningless. Third, I want you to listen. Listen to God to let Him direct your paths. The more you listen to Him, the wiser you'll become. Never doubt His love and direction for you. He is your greatest resource." These words of wisdom stood me in good stead over the twenty years we called Suriname home. I'm sure my parents gave me similar advice growing up but I wasn't ready to hear it.

I grew up assuming our family was normal, however, I think that many families are dysfunctional, even in small ways. The family I grew up in was no exception but that rarely crossed my mind as a youngster. We are imperfect people after all, and families bear imperfect characteristics.

The reader will discover that my father had many faults but he was also a man who had his good side. He taught us the value of money, how to act politely, care for one's belongings, and practice good manners. He set up savings accounts for each one of us, accounts that we were responsible to manage. He was always well dressed, and faithful in his job, to the point of crossing the picket line and being called a scab, when a union-led strike was on at the plant.

The darker side of my father's character affected us as a family, my mother in particular. The lighter side meant trips to Niagara Falls and the Detroit Zoo, for example. Dad loved to travel in the car that took our immigrant family five years to acquire.

Over time Dad grew frustrated with his own lack of accomplishments, but when he 'got religion', the family became polarized with Dad squaring off on one side and Mom and the kids on the other. It was not healthy. Dad was angry and Mom tried to protect us from that anger.

Breaking that cycle characterizes this book. To watch God accomplish great things in our lives is powerful. And to see *how* He does this, is inspiring. God demonstrates his faithfulness time and time again. To rise above that pressed down feeling is to say that God is at work, constantly.

This book is not a manual about forgiveness, neither is it a guidebook on dealing with bitterness, nor a handbook designed to work through feelings of inferiority, nevertheless, examples of all three can be found throughout its pages. God is relentlessly at work, doing what He does best: offering hope, reconciliation, and renewed life.

It's not easy overcoming the odds that we battle against and frequently it takes drastic action on our part, initiated and spearheaded with God's grace and direction, to change the course. Sometimes it means to 'burn your bed', as my mother would say. Sacrifices have to be made. It may mean working instead of sleeping. It may mean going without for a period of time to accomplish a greater good. It might also mean that we are to burn our bridges behind us, and move forward with resolution and purpose.

What surprises me is how God directs it all. The path He took me on through my first fifty years of life astonishes me, culminating in the year 2000 with the dedication of the New Testament in Suriname Javanese. To a young boy, that dream seemed impossible and implausible. But it is a fact.

The Suriname Javanese Church (Gemeente Dian) comprises at least sixteen churches, with additional congregations in The Netherlands and the Dutch Antilles using the Suriname Javanese New Testament. Many people contributed to that reality. The Old Testament translation is underway. God is not finished with this people group, nor the 1800 languages still needing Bible translation. Linda and I are grateful to be a part of something that's larger than we are, and that we are allowed to make a contribution to it.

Before I started writing, I assumed the book's title was going to be "From 0 to 500 in 50" because it focused on the comments my dad made to me as a youngster and that our translated New Testament was celebrated as the 500th when I turned 50. But as I continued to write, my mother's words "Burn your bed" kept coming back. I was standing on the front steps of our country farmhouse, on the verge of leaving for Dallas to begin my linguistics studies, when she uttered those powerful words. I understood immediately what she meant. God had clearly called me to this new venture and Mom never doubted that. If I was to burn my bed, it meant forget about sleep, study hard, and prove God strong. She was absolutely correct. It was Linda who suggested the title. The woman God gave me for a spouse was speaking with wisdom, love, and insight. Sit back and enjoy God's steady hand at work.

Are you Hiding any Jews?

It was March 1944 when the sound of hob-nailed boots echoed up and down the cobblestone streets of the quiet Dutch village. The boots stopped in front of a door and were followed by a loud rap. The 30-year-old single woman behind that door quietly shot up a short prayer, as was her habit. "Lord, please help me not to tell a lie." She swung the heavy door open and looked into the steel-blue eyes of two Dutch policemen hired by the Gestapo to fulfill their deadly orders. "Are you hiding any Jews?" they menacingly asked. Looking into their eyes she said, "Yes."

They glanced at each other, not quite sure what to make of her answer. They asked the question again, "Woman, we don't have time for jokes. Are you hiding any Jews?" The woman prayed silently, "Lord, if they cross the threshold, I won't know what to do." She looked into their eyes again and said, "Yes." The policemen turned to each other in disbelief, clicked their heels, wheeled around, and walked down the street; their boots echoing behind them. The woman, trembling, pushed the door closed and collapsed on the floor and sobbed. Indeed, she was hiding a Jewish doctor and his wife in the attic.

The war ended, she married on July 4, 1945 and had two sons. Shortly after becoming pregnant with her third child, her mother was diagnosed with cancer. As a young girl, she had often prayed that she might become a missionary nurse; the possibility of that happening seemed to be slipping through her fingers. She prayed, "Lord, I dedicate all my children to your service; those you've already given me and those unborn." As the cancer worsened, she knew her mother wouldn't be long for this world.

On a cold and snowy December day, she stood, eight months pregnant, at her mother's grave and released her into the cold, dark foreboding earth. In her grief she thought, "I'll never carry this child to term; please help me Lord." And then, on a frigid day in January 1950, my mother gave birth to me in the living room of a postwar row-housing unit. Four years later my sister was born. She would become a nurse, and I would become a missionary.

Finding the One in Forty

Twenty-nine years later, my wife Linda and I set foot on Suriname's shore. It was 1979. John Waller, the director of the Summer Institute of Linguistics (SIL) work there, made a remark that would impact our lives. "Welcome to Suriname." he said "Most of the Javanese people live along the coast, spread over some 40 villages. Find a village to live in to learn their language and culture." We were stunned. How do we go about 'finding a village to live in' if we don't even know a single word of the language? How do we tell the difference between the Javanese and all the other ethnic groups that call Suriname 'home'?

But start we did. We quickly discovered that the Javanese set up food stands in the capital city of Paramaribo on the weekends. Every Friday and Saturday night we trolled the city for the best Indonesian food in all of South America. We settled upon one particular food stand that drew us back almost every single weekend and quickly became friends with the owners, Marius and Kati. One Friday evening we asked them, "You understand that we've come to Suriname to learn the Javanese language and culture. Can you suggest a village that we could live in to accomplish that?" Marius replied, "My uncle is a lurah, a headman of a village called Dessa. Let's go there and ask him."

The following week the four of us drove out to the lurah's home in the small village of Dessa. Although the community was only 30 minutes from Paramaribo (on a good day, when it wasn't raining and the road was passable), it was easily a hundred years removed from Paramaribo, in terms of services available and ease of access. After many rounds of overly sweet tea, snacks, and pleasantries, we made our desires known to the lurah. The lurah, however, quickly made it clear that he wasn't the one who could make that decision. "Only the Islamic priests at the mosque can do that. I'll ask them," he said. What chance was there that a white Christian couple would be permitted to live in a Muslim village? Precious little, we reasoned.

Several long weeks went by. Our prayer partners and SIL colleagues were alerted and joined us in prayer. On the weekend we found ourselves back at the food stand, and Marius greeted us with these

Our village house, before starting repairs

unexpected but welcome words, "The priests have met; they have granted you permission to live in their village. They've also found a house for you to rent." Wonder of wonders!

For the next few months, countless trips were made to Dessa, painting and repairing our 16' x 20' home. Dessa meant 'village' in the language, and with its 500 inhabitants, would become our new home. Expanding the little wooden structure by adding a kitchen, a utility room, and an indoor bathroom, were high on the to-do list. We dreaded the thought of having to use an outhouse. Maintaining one meant moving it frequently. With the good help from Buck, our Guyanese worker hired by SIL, we dug a hole for a septic tank, allowing us to have indoor plumbing. Our sanity, at least in part, was preserved.

A few weeks before starting construction I was standing by the shallow well that was some 50 feet from the house. Every home had its own well. Proximity to the Atlantic Ocean meant that the water table was extremely high and water was easily available. Thankfully the well had already been dug and was in place. The challenge facing us was getting the water to the house. I grabbed a galvanized steel bucket and lowered it by the flimsy rope tied to its handle. As it landed on the water 15 feet below, I shook the rope vigorously but the bucket refused to tip over. When I pulled it up it was only half full. While I was holding the bucket, I heard the laughter of children behind me. Two girls, ages 5 or 6, stood there giggling. The language was still foreign to us and I had no idea what they were saying. They came closer to the well and one of them took the bucket, dumped out the pathetic little bit of water and walked to the well. She turned the bucket upside down, letting it fall into the well, still holding onto the rope. It hit the water with a resounding thud that echoed softly up the cement walls, and turned over instantly. Expertly pulling it up by the rope, she turned and handed the now overflowing bucket to me. I was transfixed, completely dumbfounded. The girls snickered, walked away arm in arm, laughing at what they had just experienced. I was left holding the rope and bucket and I cried. In less than two minutes I had been reduced to the level of a child in this language and culture. Was I ready for this?

In the ensuing weeks I bought an electric shallow water pump and some PVC piping, dug a trench and buried the piping and electric line in the soft, sandy soil. In two days we went from a metal bucket to turning on a tap in the house, saving ourselves countless hours of heavy work. Thankfully electricity was available most of the time in Dessa, even if it meant having only 15 amps of service.

Three weeks after settling into the house, a woman came by and said quietly, "Ed and Linda, did you know that there is a Christian church in our village?" I clearly remember looking at Linda and then at the woman, stunned by her words. No, there wasn't a church in our village. There must be some mistake. Everyone knew where the mosque was located because the call to prayer could be heard five times per day. "What do you mean to say that there is a Christian church in our village?" She insisted on showing us. She took us by the hand and led us a short distance down the dusty, sandy road, right past the mosque. We turned left and there, perched in between two houses, was a building smaller than our house. Over the doorway hung a weathered wooden sign that read "Pasamuan Kristen" or, Christian congregation. We looked at each other in total disbelief. A Christian church in an Islamic village? How was it possible? "Yes," she said, "people meet here every Sunday evening at 6:00 P.M. You might want to come next week."

Months later we discovered that of all the 40 villages dotting the northern coast of Suriname where the Javanese lived, Dessa was the only one that had a Christian church using the language as it was spoken by the people.

Is That Allowed?

Awarm and muggy evening was in store for us as walked the dusty, road to the one-room village church. We ambled past the mosque on our right and could see the church on the left. How was it possible that a church had been built within a stone's throw of the all-imposing mosque? We would discover the miracle of that later on. We were still a hundred yards away but already the singing from the small gathering was filtering through the jungle trees. Upon entering the building I noticed two dim fluorescent bulbs hanging from the ceiling. The walls were mere slats, allowing the tropical breeze to push through the building, stirring up mosquitoes and bats alike, swooping over us through the humid air. Several hard, whitewashed benches were scattered around the perimeter. A small wooden music stand stood on the raised podium. There were no more than ten people present but they were eagerly greeting each other in their mother tongue.

A young man strolled in, playing a guitar, singing in the language. The gathering burst into song followed by prayer that was likewise in the local language. But we didn't understand a word of it. It would be a while before we did. The language was completely unwritten and the songs had been memorized. As the group settled down for the message, I noticed that the leader pulled out two Bibles. He read a passage from Matthew 6 in the Indonesian Bible. The reading of the Scripture passage was met by blank stares of incomprehension. I thought, "Surely these people must understand some of this. They came, after all, from Indonesia to this far flung land on the South American continent only 120 years ago."

Next, Antoon, the leader, read the identical passage from the Dutch Bible, Suriname's national language. More blanks stares. I thought, "Yes, countries can make their national language anything they want; that doesn't mean that people will automatically speak it or understand it." He closed the two Bibles, laid them aside and launched into a short sermon. "Here's what these passages mean in our language," he said. Suddenly the small crowd woke up, nodding in agreement with every word that was spoken. It was obvious that the little group was enjoying this. We, however, were clueless what was being said but we understood only too well, linguistically, what was taking place. Sweat droplets formed on my upper lip as the humidity slowly increased throughout the evening, here on the northernmost edge of the Amazon rainforest.

I listened carefully, trying to pick up a few words here and there. One thing was certain: this weekly meeting would be a rich place for language learning.

We returned to the place week after week, building our friendship and our vocabulary. It occurred to me to talk to Antoon about the weekly choreography he performed with his Bibles. One evening I approached him after the service and asked, "Antoon, every week you go through the routine of using two Bibles followed by doing a translation on the fly so your people can understand the message." "Yes," he said, "what choice do I have?" "We could help you translate the Scriptures into the language of your people." He turned and gave me the most incredulous look. "Would that be allowed?" he questioned.

My mind raced back to my childhood days. My mother had always read to us from a children's Bible. As children we had memorized many of the stories. "Well," I said, "I don't know if it's allowed or disallowed, but let's conduct an experiment. What if we took some Genesis stories and did a children's version of them." I suggested we could start with Adam and Eve in the Garden of Eden, Cain and Abel, the Tower of Babel, and Noah and the Flood. It was best to conduct the test in a different village where the people were more likely to be unacquainted with the material. If people who were initially ignorant of the content can understand the stories, then almost anyone in the 40 villages can understand them. Antoon agreed.

I said, "Contact me when you think you're ready to start and we'll go from there. In the meantime, we'll be right here in the village, developing the writing system, doing an initial grammar analysis, and increasing our fluency."

Renewed expectancy was in the air. Our fluency was slowly increasing; we were able to make short conversational visits with village neighbors. The discovery of the tiny Christian church encouraged us and the thought that initial Bible translation might start soon drove us on. Little did we know that the wait for Antoon to announce his readiness would be painful and long. Nor did we know what would precipitate his announcement.

Newly arrived and ready to start

When Do We Start?

It was April 1983 and our first furlough was fast approaching. Excitement was building in our little household as we anticipated heading back to North America to see family, friends, and the churches that had sent us four years earlier. David, our firstborn, was already two-and-a-half years old and most of our family had not yet seen him. Nephews and nieces born during our absence were names on telegrams or pictures and we were anxious to get caught up and acquainted. There definitely seemed to be a price to pay for living overseas, and it was a price that both sides of our families paid.

I felt like the apostle Paul, reporting back to the churches about his journeys, frustrations, and accomplishments. Yet, I felt like I had little to report after those first four years. Back in the village we had established an initial working alphabet for the Suriname Javanese language. Our first booklet, the Christmas Story, had just been published. We titled it "Lairé Jésoes" or "The Birth of Jesus". Its light green cover conveyed a sense of accomplishment. The booklet, replete with illustrations from the David C. Cook Foundation, was ready for distribution. Antoon had not been part of the project. He was a school teacher in another village, using Dutch as the vehicle for instruction. He was a busy man, as a full-time teacher and shepherding the weekend flock in Dessa. When he saw the publication he bristled. I knew he was displeased simply by the way he leafed through its pages.

It had been 3½ years since we first met in the village church when Antoon announced his decision to get involved in the Genesis stories. "Okay," he said, "I think I'm ready to start."

Since we were a couple of months away from our furlough, there didn't seem to be sufficient time to conduct the Genesis stories experiment. Let's wait until we get back, I reasoned. But another thought struck me that said I should strike while the iron was still hot. "Okay," I said, "let's meet in my office in the morning and begin."

Together, we worked on the stories, using the best translation principles we had. In a couple of weeks we were armed with the resulting stories, extra copies made using carbon paper. The age of computers and digital printers was dawning but had not yet fully arrived. The copies had been printed using an IBM Selectric with its rotating type balls spinning and whirring across the pages.

We drove to the Suriname River which could only be crossed using an old ferry to get to the village. There, we would put our stories to the test. The 45-minute boat ride always seemed interminably long. We deliberately chose to avoid it as much as possible. When we got to the other side of the river we had another 30-minute drive to the Javanese village of Tamanredjo. Arrangements had been made for our arrival and a small group of Javanese had gathered for the evening event. I wondered if it would work or if we could find anyone to read the material? Only a few people out of the 60,000 Suriname Javanese had ever seen anything in print in their own language and not one of them lived in this village.

Antoon asked if there were any volunteers to read one of the stories. A young boy 11 or 12 years old offered. In almost flawless form, he read through the story of Cain and Abel. I was stunned. Maybe our orthography was better than what we had originally thought. The boy, like many others gathered that evening, had been schooled in Dutch and had learned to read in a language that wasn't his first. Antoon nudged me, "Yes, he's one of the brighter ones." We continued with the other stories. Some people chose to read while others preferred to listen. Then it was the time for our question and answer period. We wanted to ask questions about the story's content to see how much was comprehended. Answers requiring a 'yes' or 'no' response were ruled off limits, as there was a 50/50 chance of people getting the right answer without understanding the question.

We began our comprehension checking with questions. Can you tell me what happened in this story? What happened next? Who was involved? How was that done? Why did such-and-such happen? These questions were designed to help us discover if the people truly understood the material or were merely guessing.

As the checking progressed, I was amazed at the level of understanding. Even those who couldn't read were answering the majority of the questions correctly. The experiment had lasted 45 minutes.

There was deadly silence in the car as Antoon and I drove back to the ferry. Not a word was exchanged. I wondered what he was thinking. We arrived at 11:00 P.M., just in time to catch the last ferry of the evening. I remember driving the car on to the steel deck. The ferry had seen better days but it was still operational. Antoon got out of his side of the car and drifted off to a far corner of the deck. I walked to a different part and put my arm on the railing, staring into the dark, murky waters of the Suriname River. The captain turned off the bright floodlight that was shining down onto the car deck. It was now almost pitch black.

The old boat heaved a little as it left the wooden dock, its powerful diesel engines purring underneath our feet. The 50 cars and their passengers would soon reach the other side and drive off to their destinations. I would be home well after midnight but it didn't matter. A warm tropical breeze drifted across my face. As I leaned on the railing, I prayed a short but silent prayer, much like my mother used to do. "Lord, when are you going to send us someone who can help us do the translation of your Word for these people?" It was a prayer I had prayed a thousand times. While I was praying, I felt a hand on my right shoulder. I thought, "Oh my goodness, it must be an angel!" Hesitantly, I turned to the right and looked into Antoon's jet black eyes. He spoke softly, just loud enough above the whirr of the diesel engines. "Ed, I can't get over what happened in that village tonight. It was amazing. To see my people reading and understanding something written in their own language was a real shock. The experiment was a huge success, and I've made a decision. I'm going to quit my day job as a teacher to come and help you do Bible translation. When do we start?" I was so surprised by his softly spoken words that I almost fell overboard. I grabbed hold of the railing and shouted, "Tomorrow. We're going to start tomorrow!"

BURN YOUR BED

Big Zero

Before I get ahead of myself, I want to take you back to my childhood, growing up in southern Ontario, where the Lord started to shape me into the person he wanted me to be. And it starts out with some really ugly and painful words. I heard them frequently.

"You're just a big zero! I can't wait until you're old enough to leave this household. When you do, I'm going to hoist the flag to the top of the highest flagpole I can find in celebration! You have nothing to contribute to this household."

I remember hearing those painful words spoken many times by my frustrated father as my siblings and I were growing up in London, Ontario. Dad would sometimes yell cruel words of frustration and anger, signifying his own unfulfilled dreams and desires. We children would cower.

I was born in January 1950, in Utrecht, the Netherlands, five years after the end of World War II. Our family lived in row housing hastily constructed at the end of the war. Zilvergeldstraat 31 is an address that is etched into my memory. That's where I was born, in the living room. In 1986, while on vacation in Europe, we found the address. It still resembled a housing project from the 1950s. We walked up to the front door and knocked. A Yugoslavian refugee opened the door. We tried talking to him, but I don't think he understood a lot of Dutch. There was no use explaining to him what had started right here back in the early 1950s. We walked away in silence. My mind vaulted back several decades, when I, as boy of 5, had gone missing in this exact same neighborhood. My mother searched frantically for me, asking neighbors to join her. They found me standing on a small island in the middle of an intersection, waving my arms like a policeman, directing traffic. Mom scooped me up into her arms, tears of joy running down her cheeks.

My two older brothers were already attending school. Our family had recently acquired an AM radio, the first of its kind, and I was memorizing the lyrics to popular Dutch songs. I waited for my brothers' favorite song to play and when it did, I quickly turned the radio off. An hour later they came home from school, and I ran to them and said, "Hey, your favorite song is on the radio. Come and listen." I turned the radio on, expecting to hear the remainder of the song when I had turned it off an hour ago, but instead, a completely different song was playing. I was so puzzled and disappointed that it took me a while to figure out that radio was live. Nothing was saved in storage. It would take years before that was possible.

When I was six, our family chose to emigrate from the Netherlands. Thousands of families had made the move west across the Atlantic Ocean, and we would follow my aunt and uncle, who had emigrated a couple of years earlier. Meaningful employment in the Netherlands was scarce and the opportunities in Canada seemed limitless. In May 1956, our family boarded a DC-6 propeller-driven piston-powered airplane for Montreal, our port of entry. The plane would eventually make stops in London, Reykjavik, Iceland, and one additional stop before landing in Montreal, Canada. There we boarded a train to Chatham, to start our new lives. I remember standing on the steps of the rollaway stairs that had been pushed up against the airliner at Schiphol Airport. We posed for pictures. I was terrified about getting on board. I thought the airplane would roll and spill the passengers out once it got into the air. I can remember clutching my mother's purse.

For nearly a year we settled as a family in Chatham before moving to London, about an hour away. The apartment in Chatham was in the upstairs of a larger apartment complex in a downtown neighborhood. It wasn't much different from the row housing we had left behind in the Netherlands, except that it was upstairs, overwhelmingly warm and extremely uncomfortable in the summertime. It had three bedrooms, a small kitchen and living space. Creaky wooden outdoor steps led to a small backyard shared by other occupants. My mother would climb those dangerous stairs to hang up the laundry to catch the morning breeze.

We quickly became known as the most recent immigrants and the fight was on. Name calling was a favorite sport of our new neighbors and we were called every name in the book during that short year. English was a brand new language for us, which we kids picked up easily but my 42-year-old mother struggled with it. Mom had sung Dutch hymns and Psalms growing up and they provided much comfort to her, especially during times of stress and discomfort. As she hung up the laundry outdoors, she could frequently be heard singing her Psalms, her alto voice carrying across the small grassy space. The neighbors would angrily yell at her, "Shut up! Shut up!" Mom had no idea what these strange words meant and she would yell right back at them, "Ja shure, shud up!" Whenever she told this story, we would laugh and cry at the same time. She was determined to keep her Lord squarely in front of her, realizing He was the one giving her daily strength and sustenance. But it hurt us to see how mother was treated. I would think, 'Were these people any different than us? Hadn't they all immigrated as well at some point in their lives? Some were probably already second generation immigrants, but many were first generation and would have experienced the same things our family was experiencing. Why did they insist on making fun of us like this?'

Slowly, my six-year-old mind wondered if perhaps there might be a better place for our family to live. Maybe a place where we could run and sing at the top of our lungs; maybe a place where we had some space to spread out and learn to be dignified human beings again. I started to pray for such a place. My prayer was simple but truthful. "Lord, I want to ask you for a place for our family that's out in the country, a place with lots of trees, a place where we can run and play, and a house that's truly big enough for all of us." I had not yet comprehended that praying such a prayer was completely foolish, an impossible prayer, but I prayed it anyway.

One morning I woke up with an extremely sore throat, complaining that I couldn't swallow. Mom reached for some cough medicine but it barely helped. A quick trip to the doctor revealed swollen tonsils and the only recommended solution back in 1957 was a tonsillectomy. Our family was terrified at the possibility of my going to the hospital. We didn't have a car. The only way to get around was to walk, use public transportation, or go by bicycle. I ended up sitting on the back of Dad's bicycle as he pedaled to the hospital, admitting me for surgery.

A big, black rubber mask was put over my face and the next thing I knew I was lying in a bed that wasn't my own. Strangers in white uniforms came and went. I was too sick to even acknowledge their presence. All day long they flitted back and forth, doing their jobs. My throat, in the meantime, was sore again, but this time because of the surgery. I felt sick to my stomach and took no pleasure in seeing or talking with anyone. When my family came to see me, I shooed them away, telling them I was unwilling to talk.

I kept praying for that house, the one with many rooms and a yard with many trees, unaware that God was already working behind the scenes. Dad received the news that there was work in another city, about 60 miles away. He would still be working in a hospital as an orderly but the chance to earn $40 per week sounded extremely appealing to him. He made a couple of visits to that city and the hospital. Before long, a large stake truck pulled up to the front door of our decrepit little apartment on Raleigh Street. It was not hard to say goodbye to the row housing, nor the neighbors; we had been treated less like humans and more like scum. But where would we move to? And what would the next dwelling look like? I was anxious, remembering the simple prayer that I had prayed repeatedly. I was afraid of being laughed at for praying that prayer but I was determined to keep on telling the Lord my desires.

After a drive that seemed to take forever, the truck chugged its way to the top of a hill that appeared long and steep, at least to this eight-year-old's mind. The fully laden truck turned into a long driveway that led to an old farmhouse that we later discovered was at least 60 years old. It appeared to be well built and sturdy. As the truck came to a stop in front of the house (it was set back from the road by at least 200 feet) I quickly realized that we were in the country. Yet, we were only five minutes from town. There were no immediate neighbors. I jumped out of the truck and ran around the perimeter of the huge property, running as fast as my legs would take me, counting the many trees. There were leafy maples, towering pines, and large elms. A whole row of conifers lined the long gravel driveway. I couldn't believe it. Eighty-four trees! There were trees to climb in, trees to swing from, and trees to shelter the old place from the winter storms that were sure to follow. I was crying like a baby when I returned to the starting point of my counting expedition. In my mind, God had answered my prayers.

The house turned out to be a drafty old thing but its sturdy hand hewn beams held it together securely. There were plenty of rooms for everyone to have their own bedroom, a small garage for a car that we were still several years away from owning, and room to grow, room to make noise outdoors, and room to plant a large garden on its two acres. That warm day in the summer of 1958, God did a miracle in a young boy's heart; He affirmed that He listens to our prayers and that He delights in answering them. Many more prayers would be prayed in that country house, some of which would impact me for a long time to come.

Leaving the Netherlands for Canada in 1956.
I'm clutching my mother's purse.

Dad Struggles

B eing called a big zero would have a powerful impact on me. I didn't realize it at the time but negative thoughts were starting to form in my young mind. Mom would tell us that Dad was frustrated because of similar happenings that took place in the Netherlands when he was a youth. We heard the story more than once about Dad's grandfather, apparently a tyrant of a man. He owned a butcher shop and his son, my grandfather, worked for him. On occasion, my great-grandfather would beat his son with a leather whip when he got out of line. My grandfather learned to resent his father for good reason. When it came time for my grandfather to choose a career, it was a natural choice to become a butcher. And his son, Alexander, my father, worked for his Dad in that butcher shop.

Love was rarely expressed in that household. The emphasis was on work, the harder the better. My grandmother didn't make the situation any better as she frequently parroted her husband's actions.

When World War II broke on European soil, Dad, who was in his early 20s, spent some time working for the underground, known as the Dutch Resistance. This Movement had thousands of members. Many of them were arrested by the occupying Germans. They, in turn, were subsequently jailed for months, tortured, sent to concentration camps or even killed. Although my Dad preferred not to talk about those days, he did tell us that he spent some time in a concentration camp. My father, who had some knowledge of food preparation because of his butcher shop experience, ended up working in the large kitchens, cooking for both the Resistance workers and the Germans alike. Every now and then the top brass would put in special orders to the kitchen for large cakes to celebrate an officer's birthday. Dad and others in the kitchen would spit into the cake batter as a way of showing their disgust for the occupying German Army. One thing was certain, working in the kitchen normally meant having sufficient to eat.

When the liberation of Holland took place by the Allied Forces, some Canadian and American forces stormed the concentration camps freeing those trapped inside. Artillery shells were fired into the camps by the Allied troops. The resistance movement members were told to get down and lie low. My Dad distinctly remembered artillery fire whizzing mere inches past his head, when he didn't react quickly enough to the order.

When liberation was complete and the war was finally over, thousands upon thousands of Dutch people returned to their communities to start the long process of rebuilding their lives. My Dad and Mom married on July 4, 1945. Work was scarce and the Dutch Government made an offer that many would quickly accept. Emigration to countries like Canada and Australia became an enticing offer that tens of thousands of Dutch people gratefully took. The thought of owning some property and starting a farm or a business was an irresistible offer. As you drive along the Niagara Escarpment in southern Ontario, you will notice many Dutch names on those farms. They also settled in other parts of Ontario and Alberta. Large farms growing wheat, barley, and oats dot the landscape in the province of Alberta. Some of the orchards in the Okanagan Valley in British Columbia also bear Dutch names. DeBoer, Brouwer, and Vanderkamp are not unusual. These productive farms were started in the 1940s and 1950s, some even earlier.

As we settled into our new home in Chatham and later London, Ontario, Dad found work in the hospitals. Those were good years. My brothers and I earned our first dollars by delivering newspapers in the nearby well-to-do neighborhood of Medway Heights, commonly referred to as Pill Hill, because so many medical doctors lived there. Our old rented farmhouse stood on the edge of that neighborhood, less than a mile away and we quickly became known as the Dutch immigrants who were willing to work hard. We mowed their lawns, shoveled their snow, delivered their newspapers, babysat their children, and Mom cleaned their fabulous homes. Among those clients was the McGregor family who owned a company that manufactured steel and copper tubing. She put in a good word with Mr. McGregor and before long Dad was employed there. Dad would also become the recipient of Mr. McGregor's expensive suits that he no longer deemed wearable. My father was always impeccably dressed for church and other functions, largely due to the fact that he and Mr. McGregor were approximately the same size.

But something was gnawing at my father's heart. To be working in a factory was only a job, not a career. Dad was an artist. He loved to draw and read. Things would frustrate him as the years slipped away, holding down a factory job with no advancement. He would talk sometimes about getting a better education. Thoughts and comments of going into the ministry also surfaced. We children were getting our own educations and Dad was feeling the frustration of being left out and left behind. The feeling of defeat would often rear its ugly head at the dinner table.

Dad complained how difficult it was to have a job that required so much physical labor. A factory-wide swing shift policy was established. The employees would work the day shift for two weeks, then two weeks in the afternoon shift, and finally two weeks in the graveyard shift. Sleep was often impossible when making the transition from one shift to another. Working the swing shift is comparable to jet lag. The challenge of trying to stay awake when the body is screaming for sleep is exasperating. Frequently Dad would yell at us children. We were easy scapegoats for his anger, and it was not uncommon to hear the term 'big zeroes' being tossed about. In all fairness to my father, his work schedule was extremely difficult, coupled with the fact that his job was on a road to nowhere.

Housing God's Creation

T he old homestead on the tree-lined property housed more than human occupants. A house this old and drafty was bound to have other creatures inhabit its warm spaces. In the wintertime we could hear the squirrels scurrying through the attic, storing up their winter morsels. We offered to seal off all the cracks that allowed them access but Mom insisted that all God's creation was to be respected and cared for. I found it hard to argue with her reasoning. Whatever leftovers there were after meals would be reheated but when we simply refused even those, they were deposited on a large stone that served as a cover for a deep well next to the house. Birds, squirrels, raccoons, and the occasional deer took advantage of this free food, especially in the wintertime.

On a summer day my brother's friend Burt showed up with his BB gun. He was going to demonstrate it to us boys. Burt lined the sight up with a squirrel sitting on a branch, took aim, fired, and instantly the helpless beast hit the ground, flailing on its way down. We ran over to the now clearly dead squirrel and properly pronounced it dead. A twinge went up my spine. Burt showed us a few more times how effective his BB gun was and what a tremendous shot he was. When Mom looked out the window and saw her sons gathered around the now growing pile of dead rodents, she ran outside, scolded Burt for harming God's creatures and sent him packing.

On yet another warm summer night we were rudely awakened by the pungent smell of a passing skunk. The odor was unmistakable and the little black and white striped beast was lingering way too close to the house. My brother decided to take matters into his own hands. He found a really large rock, larger than he could comfortably carry, and climbed to the roof. We handed him the rock and he carried it to the edge of the roof. When the skunk roamed closer to the house, he took careful aim and launched the projectile in the direction of the unsuspecting creature. We had our own way of taking care of unwanted animals but the price we paid that night was a high one. The skunk exploded and the overpowering odor lingered, making sleep all the harder for the next several days. Mom lamented this kind of action but held back her comments.

Wild blackberries and black raspberries grew along the fence of our two-acre property. In the early morning before breakfast, Mom could often be found perusing the fence in search of those little delicacies, her unmistakable alto voice giving away her location. Some of our Pill Hill neighbors had apple trees in their front yards. On her way to work, Mom would gather up some of the apples that had fallen to the ground, apples that surely would rot and never be eaten. The homeowner noticed my Mom gathering up the apples and scolded her. She quietly walked away, went home, made applesauce and walked back to the owner's home and presented him with a jar of the homemade goodness. He was completely caught off guard by Mom's humble act and invited her to come back anytime to gather up the dropped fruit.

Flying Gravel

We loved being in our brightly painted cozy kitchen that served as the dining room, homework room, undeniably the most comfortable room in the aging farmhouse. The potbellied stove that stood next to the outside wall was spreading its warming rays throughout the room. We sometimes engaged Dad in discussion in that kitchen. He had become dissatisfied with the church we were attending and decided on a new course of action.

When Dad 'got religion' he started church hopping, in search of one that he agreed with. When he finally settled on one, he tried to convince the rest of the family to join him. He reasoned that the old church wouldn't understand what had happened to him. He said that the rest of us were now attending a false church that was no longer preaching the true gospel. We contended that our church was preaching the truth but he didn't have ears to hear it. These short, heated discussions usually ended in stalemates.

Years earlier Dad had started to listen to some radio broadcasts that included faith healers and radio evangelists. Magazines flooded our home and sermonettes followed in their wake. We would sit uncomfortably at the dinner table on a nightly basis waiting for the next installment of Dad's new religious discoveries. It became painful night after night to be bombarded with the latest news from these radio voices. Dad had his own way of making us feel guilty about our current beliefs and conveniently assigned all of us to a place in the utter darkness if we didn't change. Blame and coercion make good bedfellows but we would have none of it.

Mom was the pillar in our household, the one who clearly displayed the most positive and humble of Christian attitudes imaginable. We saw the daily sacrifices she made for the entire family. She worked hard for 'her ladies', cleaning their lavish homes. It was her idea to take in university students to supplement the family's earnings. On weekends she cleaned doctors' offices and help Dad with the janitorial work at the local Christian school. With the additional income, she bought groceries that Dad simply refused to purchase, claiming they were unnecessary and expensive. Predictably, however, he was always the first to help himself to generous portions of the delicious scrambled eggs and Canadian bacon that made up our customary Saturday evening meal, food that Mom had bought with her hard-won earnings.

When I turned sixteen, Dad was in the middle of his newfound religiosity and insisted on making a trip to Pittsburgh, Pennsylvania to see the faith healer during one of her crusades. He invited me to go along and the two of us made our way across the border to the Steel City to hear her preach spellbinding messages about miraculous healing. Halfway through one of the services, she called my Dad and me to the podium. I asked myself, "How does she know we're here? Does she have some kind of special knowledge that the rest of us don't have?" I later found out that Dad had written to her personally to inform her of our coming to Pennsylvania on this exact day. She started, "There's a man and his young son in the audience this morning, who have come from Canada to be with us. Would you two please come forward?" I was clearly shocked by this announcement but walked up the steps to meet her. She was dressed in a long, flowing white chiffon dress. I was embarrassed to have been forced into this uncomfortable situation. Two large men dressed in suits came and took their place behind us, should we keel over when the Spirit descended on us. I noticed that many of the people that she called up had already suffered the same fate. This was clearly new territory for me. She placed one hand on my father's head and her other hand on mine and started to pray fervently for the marriage that was in so much trouble. Again, I thought, "How does she know all this?" Dad had obviously written to her and explained all about his 'unbelieving' wife, but it was never talked about in the home. Maybe he was hoping for some kind of miracle that Mom would leave her present church and join Dad in his new church. This remained a loggerheads issue throughout the latter years of the marriage.

By now I could feel the men inching closer to us, their large hands ready to catch us should we be overcome by the Spirit. I consciously spread my feet a little, determined not to fall over backwards into the waiting arms of the two eager men. She continued to pray earnestly but to no avail. After a few minutes she said amen and dismissed us to our seats, much to the disappointment of the many who had come to see others being slain in the Spirit. Red-faced I returned to my seat, unsure of what had just happened. I never did talk to my Dad about it but he seemed to have experienced something that left a deep impression on him. I think he was more determined than ever to have some type of spiritual experience and nothing was going to stand in his way, not his wife, not his children, not his job, nothing.

When we returned from our weekend excursion, Dad's attitude became more belligerent and intolerant. He stepped up his preaching at the supper table and we kids sat quietly enduring the dreaded nightly barrage. But there was no joy in it and no joy in the family. The toll it was having was undeniable and deadly.

Whenever we attempted to talk to Dad about the issues facing our family, his reaction was swift and predictable. He stood up, pulled himself to his full 6'-2" stature, glared at us, and blurted out in anger and frustration, "Who are you to tell me what to do? Who are you? You're mere children. You don't tell me what to do. I am the head of this household and I make the decisions. As for you, you are all big zeroes and you have nothing to bring into this household. When you leave this place, I'm going to hoist the flag to the top of the tallest flagpole I can find in celebration of your departure!" The words were sounding all too familiar.

With that, he would stride out of the kitchen to the garage, get into his car and drive like a wild man down the gravel driveway, dust and stones flying everywhere. It was his usual answer and practice when he was questioned about the issues that really mattered. It would be several hours before he would return, the anger and redness now flushed from his face. We normally endured the silent treatment from him for several days after these ordeals but the issues remained unresolved, festering like an untreated wound. Sooner or later, something would have to snap. And when it did, there would be a huge change in our family's life. How long would it be before this lethal ball exploded?

BURN YOUR BED

King's Kids

Our hilltop home in London turned into a greater blessing than we even imagined. Hospitality and generosity were the keywords around our old rented farmhouse. Mom knew how to decorate on a dime and found old treasures here and there that she managed to lug home. An old, discarded chair became useful once again with a little paint. I remember she brought home an old basketball hoop. Dad nailed some scrap plywood together, fastened the hoop to it, and hoisted the contraption up a tree near the end of the gravel driveway. We played for hours with our new toy.

Living on the edge of our well-to-do neighborhood had certain advantages. We descended on the area on collection day when discarded items could be picked over before the big trucks arrived. We bicycled through the neighborhood watching for the next treasure to appear.

Mom easily found jobs cleaning homes and before long she was employed five days a week. She became known as the go-to cleaning lady. She had a way with people that made up for her lack of knowledge about the English language. She had learned kindness and hospitality while hiding Jews during World War II. As an in-house nanny for Jewish families in the Netherlands, she became knowledgeable about the fine art of setting a table, waiting on dinner guests, cooking and baking, and how to make people feel at ease. She was quick to make conversation with them and people loved having her around. Frequently she would be invited by 'her ladies', as she called them, to help at the various functions held in the homes of Pill Hill residents. Whether it was a dinner party or a graduation ceremony, she mingled easily with the many guests, gracefully carrying out her art. The extra income was a wonderful bonus for our struggling immigrant family of six.

She frequently saw the dark side as well. Sometimes the doctors would be too inebriated to make it to their bedrooms and Mom would help carry them upstairs. She observed the family issues, the squabbling, and internal conflicts that find their way into the home. She sang her Dutch psalms and hymns wherever she worked; she knew that her help was in the Lord. In her broken English she would tell her ladies about the wonderful relationship that could be had knowing Jesus. They would listen politely and frequently ask for her advice about some family issue or problem. Mom would often manage to turn these conversations into opportunities to talk about her Lord.

She was always home in time to make supper for the family. When we came home from school, my brother and I would make our rounds delivering the London Free Press. Around the dinner table, Mom would tell us about her day and ask us about our experiences at school. She taught us proper etiquette and manners. She would say, "When you address your newspaper customers, learn their names and always speak with two words. Learn to say, 'Yes, Mr. Paxton', or 'Thank you, Dr. Christie', or 'Please, Mrs. Dailey.'" Politeness meant putting the other person ahead of yourself. 'John and I' was the proper form, not, 'Me and John.' Respect for others meant mentioning their name first followed by your own.

At dinnertime Mom would recall a certain conversation she had with one of her ladies or recount an experience she had while helping to cater an event. She saw the details of the families' lives and would teach us perspective by saying, "You kids need not be jealous of our rich neighbors. I see what goes on in their households, and it's often not pleasant. Just remember this; we may not have much but you are King's Kids!" Those are words we would not easily forget.

We were frequently reminded that true happiness lay in helping someone. When missionaries traveled through the area, we would host them, sometimes for days on end. We children would huddle around the guest after dinner, spellbound by their fascinating stories. One missionary told a story that demonstrated God's steadfast provision.

Hank was a traveling missionary who made the rounds visiting people in the province of Manitoba. One evening, he heard God telling him that he had to travel to another town that same evening, some three hundred miles away. He hopped into his car and partway into the trip, noticed that his gas tank was nearly empty. This was long before the days of 24-hour gas stations. The needle crept closer and closer to 'E' but he kept going. He prayed, "Lord, if you want me there, you'll have to provide because there's not a single gas station open between here and Winnipeg." With the needle stuck on empty, Hank drove through the night, witnessing the miracle as it unfolded. In the early morning hours, he reached his destination, and when he pulled his car into the driveway, it sputtered and died. As kids, we sat raptured by his story and begged for more.

Through the years, Hank and others would frequent our home. Seeds were being planted in my young mind about doing missionary work. I reasoned, 'If God can do this for people like Hank, why couldn't he do it for me?' Missionary work started to look like a real possibility, but how does one get there? What do you need to do or study to become one? I would find out on a particular trip to Mexico.

BURN YOUR BED

Mother's Message

In 1986, while visiting an outdoor museum in Enkhuizen, the Netherlands, my mother blurted out, "Oh Tryn, the potatoes need to be peeled." At first I didn't understand the statement because it was spoken in the language used in Groningen, a northern province of the Netherlands. My mother caught herself. She had slipped into her native tongue as she viewed the kitchen and the bed stay in the sod house on display in the museum. Seeing the kitchen table brought back a distant memory, when she, as a two-year-old, was told to sit under the table to peel potatoes. Language resides deep within our subconscious, and a certain smell, scene, or other mechanism can trigger powerful memories in a split second that can transport us back to another time and place. We observed my mother, grappling with the memory that had just been evoked by that seemingly innocuous kitchen table.

Mom was born in 1913 in Stadskanaal, a small town in the province of Groningen. Her father was a carpenter and a bricklayer who worked hard to support his family of nine. Mom was the second oldest child and the oldest girl and much was expected of her at a young age. With a growing family, the duties of helping her mother were quickly thrust upon her. Schooling was considered optional. Frequently as a young girl, she would slip out the back door and run towards school. Even more frequently her mother would call out the back door, "Tryn, there's far too much work today in the house. Come back and help me, right now! You can start by peeling the potatoes." Mom would disappointedly turn around and head back to the house to appease her often ill mother.

Her Dad, in the meantime, was robust, loving, and gregarious. He used his massive hands to lay bricks but those same hands became tender instruments of love as he cradled his children in his arms. Grandfather apprenticed his young sons in the art of bricklaying. Once, when he and his son were on a wooden scaffold, high above the ground, his son stepped back ever so slightly to retrieve another brick. He slipped off the edge of the wobbly platform and immediately plummeted towards the hard earth below. Grandfather saw it and called out loudly, "Lord, my son!" An errant piece of lumber, sticking out of the scaffold, expertly snagged my uncle's belt and he hung there between heaven and earth for several perilous minutes before grandpa retrieved his son, visibly shaken but ever so grateful to be alive. In an instant, God had answered the prayer.

That's the way he lived. He was a man full of faith that did not go unnoticed by my mother who started memorizing the Psalms at an early age and would quietly sing them, particularly when no one was around. They became her constant guide and companion. When we immigrated to Canada she learned them in English and could be heard singing them in two languages.

Mom's faith in the Scriptures was unshakeable. She was asked if she believed that Jonah had been swallowed by a large fish and she replied, "I believe the Bible to be accurate and truthful. In fact, if the Bible had said that Jonah swallowed the fish instead, I would still believe it."

Our old Canadian farmhouse became a haven. Not more than a quarter mile away, a narrow country lane wandered through the fields of the surrounding farm. Part of the one-lane dirt track was lined with irresistible cherry trees that would display their glorious, fragrant blossoms each spring. Shortly thereafter, delicious fruit would hang enticingly for anyone who happened to walk by. The farm, largely abandoned by now, had fallen into disuse but the trees were still fair game for our family. Cherry lane was more than just a place to gather cherries; it became a quiet and comforting place of solace for Mom, who often walked its length, pouring her heart out to the Lord, or where life's problems were discussed with us children. Trouble at school, a relationship with a girlfriend, or any situation that confronted us in life seemed to be fair game on cherry lane. If we couldn't find Mom, we knew she would be walking there, seeking wisdom from on high.

The farmhouse was well constructed but also showed its age. The house rested on square hand-hewn logs, some as much as ten inches across. These, along with smaller beams, rested on a foundation that had been built out of large stones cemented together. A small, wooden door that led to a coal chute projected out of the west side of the house next to the driveway. Several times a year, a coal truck would pull up and unload its cargo. We loved the sound of the coal sliding down the chute into the bin. Shortly after the now-coal-smeared-faces of the delivery men backed down the driveway, fine coal dust settled on virtually every horizontal surface within the home. It would be almost ten years before that coal furnace, with its octopus-like heating ducts running through the dank basement, would be replaced with a newer, modern, oil-fired furnace.

We would often hear Mom, in the dead of winter, slipping down to the basement at two or three o'clock in the morning, to stoke the furnace and restore some heat to the house. It became the job of us children to take out the ashes on a regular basis and dump them outside on an ever-growing ash heap. More dust. Many days the temperature in my upstairs bedroom would plummet to freezing during the long Canadian winters. Ice would form on the uninsulated windows and one learned not to move around in bed too much in fear of encountering yet another cold spot under the woolen blankets. It was challenging to try and heat a home with a coal furnace that relied on the thermodynamic principle that heat rose. That theory was frequently tested in our country home. The newer oil furnace was a welcome addition to the old homestead.

Breakfast usually consisted of eggs, bacon, toast, oatmeal or porridge with large doses of milk. John, the milkman, would stride into our home, carrying the large glass gallon bottles and deposit them into the refrigerator. He often commented that we were his best customer, including all those that lived in Pill Hill.

When we came home from school, Mom was already in the kitchen preparing supper as we went off to deliver our newspapers to customers who would be waiting eagerly to find out what the London Free Press had to declare on its pages.

As mentioned earlier, Mom took in university students supplying them with room and board to augment the family's income. For many years, boarders and books filled our now-overflowing home. One late afternoon, after paper delivery was complete but before supper was

39

served, Darren, one of the boarders, gathered us boys and opened up a forbidden *Playboy* magazine. We sat totally transfixed. I was the youngest of three boys and at age eleven, these images were clearly leaving an impression on me. As he paged through the magazine, we sat speechless. Just then, the bedroom door opened and Mom walked in, ready to invite us to dinner. Darren tried to hide the magazine but the damage had been done. Mom turned around, and without a word, went downstairs to the kitchen. Several minutes later we all sat at the dinner table, uncertain of what would happen next. Shortly after the first bites had been taken, Mom directed a single question towards him, "Darren, have I ever put poison in your food?" Darren, sheepishly answered, "No, madam." "Then don't put poison in my sons' minds." The matter was never spoken about again but the message was clear.

A Big Red F

The house on the hill would be our family's home throughout grade school and high school. One summer day I was delivering newspapers when I chanced upon a man working by himself in a large hole that had been dug for a new home being built in Pill Hill. I introduced myself to Gordon. His Welsh accent was unmistakable and I took an immediate liking to him. When he saw that I was the newspaper boy, he asked, "Do you live nearby?" "Yes sir," I answered, "just about a mile down the road." "How old are you, son?" "I'm 16, sir," I replied. "Are you looking for work?" "Well, sir, I hadn't thought of asking but are you offering me a job?" "Yes," he said, "why don't you show up here in the morning and I'd be happy to introduce you to my boss."

I delivered the rest of my papers as quickly as I could and pedaled home faster than my legs had ever carried me. Exhausted and out of breath, I ran into the kitchen announcing my good news. The next morning I mounted my trusty Raleigh and pedaled as fast as I could to the house under construction. Ivan, the boss, and I talked for a few minutes and he decided that as soon as the foundation was in place, I should show up with a hammer and a nail apron. Every day I biked past that soon-to-be-built house making my rounds, anxiously awaiting the day. When the day finally dawned, I was ready to learn my new trade, home-building. My first order was, "Spike that joist down." I wondered what that meant. The puzzled look on my face gave my ignorance away. "Nail that board down," I was told, "and use those 4 inch spikes, OK?" Now I understood. Gradually, over the summer, my knowledge and skill increased. Little did I know that my experience in the summer of 1966 would lead to a lifetime of loving wood and construction, standing me in good stead once I got to the mission field.

High school was not my favorite occupation, and it mistakenly reinforced some strong feelings that academics was not my strong suit. Sitting through another boring history lesson was not my cup of tea. I would much rather get up on a roof and nail down some plywood or deliver newspapers and earn some cash. There, at least, people appreciated my efforts. I enjoyed the sciences but the arts left me bored. I vividly remember an event that confirmed my mistaken thinking. I had taken a science exam and the following day as the teacher was handing back the graded papers, he slammed mine down on my desk and yelled, "When are you going to learn, Ed?" A quick glance on the front of my returned exam confirmed my deepest suspicion. A big red 'F'. I was shaking like a leaf. My thoughts immediately shot back to my Dad's ranting and raving, calling me a big zero. Maybe he was right. Maybe my teacher was right. Maybe I just couldn't cut it. Maybe it just wasn't meant to be. Swinging a hammer was an honorable occupation, after all, and I could easily make a decent living doing so. The teacher who had embarrassed me in front of my classmates suggested I go to a technical school and learn a skill or a trade.

But my Mom thought differently. She remembered what had happened in my grade school years, and reminded me of those events. When we immigrated to Canada, I had been put in the first grade. English came easily to us children and schoolwork, likewise, was not much of a challenge. At the end of the year, my parents were asked to come to the school. The teacher told them I was precocious and it would be a good idea for me to advance to the third grade in the fall, skipping over the second. That turned out to be a bad idea. Danger was looming.

Mom always read stories to us, at bedtime and sometimes during the day. As children we relished these special times. In large part it was due to Mom taking on the voice of the character. She read with deep expression, and we could always hear their voices as Mom read. When I was in the third grade reading class, the teacher picked up on that and she said, "Class, listen carefully while Edward reads the story. I want you to learn to read in this way." I thought nothing of it. I was merely emulating Mom's reading style. Within days the teacher marched me up to the fifth grade reading class and had me repeat the little experiment.

I remember the story I read that day. A hiker had become lost and trapped while traversing a canyon. The only way to extract the stranded hiker was to bring in a helicopter and airlift him out. As I read the story, I conveyed the fear that the hiker was feeling. The little helicopter came and, with a soothing voice, reassured the hiker that everything would be alright. As the story concluded, the impact of the event was not lost on me.

I was blessed with an extremely clear voice and loved to sing, already as a young child. The music teacher noticed and recommended to my parents that I sign up for a boys' choir. I would be singing descant, a coveted position for any young singer. The lack of family transportation, however, prevented my joining such an elite group.

We switched schools in the seventh grade, and my grades started to take a turn for the worse. Eighth grade proved to be a disastrous year. The teacher in those grades was also the school principal and a stern taskmaster. Everyone, including me, cringed under his watchful eye. I was distracted most of the time, too. Today, I would have been labeled ADD (Attention Deficit Disorder) but those labels didn't exist back in the 1960s. I struggled through the ninth grade. At the end of tenth grade, I was handed a failing report card and told that I would have to repeat the grade. A later analysis concluded that skipping over the second grade had been detrimental to my education and I was now paying the price. Perhaps the tension in the home was having its effect on me as well. Dad was restless. There were signs that Mom and Dad didn't always see eye-to-eye and small cracks were starting to appear. My personal motivation was at an all-time low. I remember going to a school counselor when I was twelve to talk about it. In our conversation I told him that I thoroughly enjoyed earning cash, by delivering newspapers or doing odd jobs. In fact, micro loans to family members became frequent. But I dared not tell my parents that I had been to the counseling office.

In the eleventh grade, the science teacher invited a guest lecturer into the classroom. He said, "Most of you will be heading to university after high school. But I want you to think beyond that. College is a stepping stone. In graduate school you'll finally be able to focus your studies and concentrate on the subject that interests you." My thoughts, however, were not on graduate school or even college. I didn't see how I could even make it out of high school. Perhaps the other teacher was right. I should pursue further education in a technical school. Did I really not have the qualifications for academic studies? My heart sank. With envy, I watched my brothers march off to college.

Tobacco Road

"It's $135. Take it or leave it," he said. I stared at the '58 Chevrolet. It wasn't the classic Impala model I had dreamed of but the two-door Bel Air with a straight six and automatic transmission. As I turned the key, a hissing sound came from the engine. When I opened the hood I found the air cleaner completely missing; not a good sign, but the price was right. I handed over the money and drove away, disheartened but thankful that I had basic transportation. I was 17 and this was my first car. I needed a car because the summer vacation had just started and my new summer job, working the afternoon shift at a manufacturing plant, required me to travel at hours when public transportation was unavailable.

Late one night, well after midnight, as I was driving home from that job, the dreaded red flashing cherry of a police cruiser caught my rearview mirror. The officer shone his flashlight into the car. "You'd better think twice about squealing your tires, OK son?" the officer said, eyeing me furtively in the dark, "just take it easy from here on in." I remember driving away wishing that my car had such capabilities.

I learned a lot about myself and the working world that summer. Although the manufacturing job only lasted a total of six weeks before a slowdown in the economy forced me to find another job, I was grateful for the experience and a peek into the window of the everyday world of working people. At the manufacturing plant the atmosphere was remarkably different from working for a Christian contractor building high end homes. Here, inappropriate language was the accepted standard. The employees stole from their employer on a regular basis.

After work one midnight, another employee invited several of us to see his car in the parking lot. When he popped the hood, we stood transfixed by a sea of chrome that met our gaze. He had taken advantage of the chroming division in the plant and methodically brought in his engine piece by piece, shoving the pieces through a small basement window to avoid detection upon entering or leaving the plant.

One employee was branded a Jesus Freak. He used his Bible as a weapon, lecturing us during break times to turn from our sins. Another worker usually arrived at four o'clock to begin his shift too drunk to work. He normally found a secluded spot somewhere, sleeping off his stupor before he returned to his work around eight o'clock.

We were paid for doing piece work. The more you produced chroming the various faucets and handles, the more you earned. This was a great incentive for me but it required the cooperation of others to see the process through. Often, after we had reached our quota for the day, I would continue mounting the articles on the chroming racks, hoping to get ahead but my fellow employees preferred to play cards the last hour or hour-and-a-half.

My carpentry job of the previous summer was still available and I easily gravitated to my hammer and nail apron. It renewed me as I loved working outdoors. The skills I was learning had unlimited value. The smell of new home construction, the sound of nails being driven into the studs, and the tremendous satisfaction of watching and participating in something useful being built, buoyed my spirit.

When the carpentry jobs gave out, my brother and I headed for the tobacco fields scattered throughout southern Ontario. This was long before the link between smoking and lung cancer/emphysema was firmly established. My job was to drive the "boat", a wooden structure with long metal runners that a strong horse pulled between the tall rows of ripening tobacco. Whenever the horse pulled in the direction away from the barn, he did so reluctantly and had to be prodded along frequently. But as soon as the horse was turned into the direction towards the barn, he pulled his increasingly heavy load with eagerness and vigor. On one occasion he pulled so hard that he broke the chain from the boat and galloped full speed for the barn. I found him standing by his stall, his head deep in a bucket of wholesome oats, ears swept back in defiance and eyeing me suspiciously, daring me to get him back to those hot tobacco fields. The farmer later told me that "the horse had smelled the barn." Later on, in Suriname, I would discover just how poignantly that phrase had been engraved into my mind.

When the picking season was over and the tobacco was hanging in the kilns to cure, the farmer invited me to spend an extra week on the farm cutting down the tobacco stalks. I was eager for the additional income and jumped at the chance.

The stalk cutter was a dangerous looking contraption with a series of six long parallel blades that rotated as it was pulled, similar to a discer or harrow when hitched to a tractor. On one occasion, a good sized rock loomed in front of the tractor. Without stopping, I jumped off but my leg caught on the brake pedal. I fell to the ground, just ahead of the tractor's large rear wheel with the stalk cutter barely six feet behind. The rear wheel ran over my right leg, pushing it into the sandy soil. The pain seared through my body but I had to get my leg out of the way of the whirring stalk cutter. I quickly extracted myself away from the slicing blades, thankful that my leg wasn't broken or that I hadn't passed out. I hastily jumped back on the tractor and turned off the ignition, starting to comprehend what had taken place. God had spared my leg and my life.

The following summer I would return to the same farm to pick the tobacco. The money was better but the work was back-breaking. School, furthermore, sounded even better than this and I was eager to return to the books. Near the end of the tobacco picking season the farmer asked us if we wanted to go to another farm to work for an additional week or two. My brother and I both agreed to the deal, and we were told that we could expect our new employer to pick us up soon.

That afternoon as we were sitting on a bench talking about what we might expect at the next farm, a pickup truck drove into the yard. We weren't totally sure if this was our new boss but it seemed unlikely that another farmer would drive in, looking for tobacco pickers. Something seemed suspicious, though. We jumped in and before long we knew that we had been hired by the wrong farmer.

There was little talk between us as we drove for about 45 minutes. When we arrived at this farmer's tobacco fields, we gave each other a wary glance. This tobacco was not in good shape and the weeds were practically choking out the crop. The farmhouse was unkempt and disorderly. Dirty dishes piled high in the sink and a most unpleasant odor hung in the air. We were barely greeted by the farmer's wife who showed us to our upstairs bedroom. The sheets on our beds were filthy. This was a far cry from the farm we had just worked at. There, the kitchen was bright, clean, and well lit. That farm was well cared for and the meals were sumptuous affairs, three times a day. In comparison, this was a most undesirable situation and we longed to be back in Tillsonburg. We were sure that we didn't want to work here but we were caught in a bind. How were we going to get out of this predicament?

We went for a walk and ended up walking right out of the driveway, hitch-hiked our way into town and arrived home two hours later. It was midnight when we saw the warm lights of our old farmhouse. Our own clean beds never looked so welcoming. Mom was absolutely delighted to see us and thankful that we were home, safe and sound. We decided that giving two summers to the nicotine patch was more than enough.

My brothers went back to college after the summer. Again, I looked on with envy.

Don't Look, Keep Going

I wondered if I would ever get the opportunity to follow them. I was apprehensive and the thought of ending up in some dead end job frightened me, staring me directly in the face. My mother's words rattled around in my mind. "Ed, have you finished your homework? Have you done all your assignments? Oh Ed, I'm so worried about you." Deep down, I knew that I was letting her and myself down. I had the capacity to do much better work, but I was unmotivated and scared at the same time.

When the opportunity came to visit my brother for a weekend, Mom, my sister, and I jumped at the chance. I came back from that trip, envious and scared. College seemed even further out of my grasp. When the school year was over, my brother chose not to come home but look for summer employment in Chicago. I was heartbroken because I had an endless amount of questions for him. We made plans that the three of us would go to Chicago to visit him. My worn-out '58 Chevy was our only means of transportation. When we told my Dad that we were planning a road trip to Illinois, he laughed at me, "That car will never make it," he mocked. I reassured him that we were going on the trip, no matter what, because we desperately wanted to see my brother.

The following morning the three of us hopped in and headed for the Windy City, some six hours away. Partway through the trip we were met with a terrific thunderstorm. These old cars had vacuum powered wipers and whenever we accelerated, the wipers would almost stop doing their job, gaining momentum as we let up on the gas. On one occasion it was raining so hard that I had to slow down to see what was ahead of us and in so doing, the wipers worked harder and faster than ever before. Suddenly, the right hand wiper flew off the arm, and we were left with barely half a windshield to look through. Other cars had pulled off the road to wait it out. We passed them and kept going. We passed other vehicles along the way, some stranded along the side of the road. Every time we encountered yet another vehicle, Mom would say, "Don't look Ed, just keep going. Keep going, Ed."

Exhausted and frazzled by the long drive, we finally pulled up to the house expecting to find my brother but the house was dark and ominous. A knock on the front door produced nothing. We walked around the back, thinking there must be another entrance and when we knocked on the back door, an elderly woman came out. When we inquired about him, she said, "Oh, I'm so sorry! Haven't you heard? He's been in a motorcycle accident and is in the hospital." We all started to cry at once at the news. What were we going to do now?

We found him in a hospital bed, bandaged up and obviously hurting. When we inquired about his condition he spoke slowly and deliberately, the anguish clearly showing on his face. He said, "A driver came across the intersection without stopping at the median and I T-boned her, flipping over her car and landing on my rear end. But I can't stay here in the hospital. I don't have any insurance. I'm incredibly sore but have no broken bones. Let's get out of here." He slowly extracted himself from the hospital bed, shuffled off to the nurses' station and with a flick of the pen, released himself from the hospital. We practically had to carry him as he hobbled down the hallway. It was agonizing to watch.

The next morning he insisted that we go to the Art Institute of Chicago. We spent several hours at the famous institution. My brother expounded on the many well-known artists and their paintings. It was as if we had our own personal tour guide. But he was clearly in much pain as he ambled through the museum. We decided it would be better that he come home with us. The following morning the four of us drove back to London and my brother spent a number of weeks recuperating until the beginning of the new college year. Right then and there I made the decision that I was going to join him, no matter what. But what lay in store for me was more than I had expected. It would be life-changing.

I limped out of high school like a bird with a broken wing and drove off to college without having applied beforehand. When I showed up to register for classes, my name wasn't on the list and was told to head off to the admissions office. There, a kind and understanding man asked me some serious questions, and allowed me to register for classes on academic probation. He instructed me to show up at his office twice a week, with all graded assignments and tests in hand. I walked out flying high but really nervous. I had been given a break, a big break, and I recognized it as such. Could I prove my high school teachers wrong? Could I make my Mom proud? Could I show my own father that I really wasn't a big zero? Could I demonstrate to myself that I wasn't as incompetent as I had painted myself to be? I didn't know the answers to my own questions. I was at a fork in the road. Was I going to accept this challenge and choose the higher road, the more difficult path, or was I going to succumb to my fears, turn around and head back home, agonizing over the fact that the challenge presented to me was too difficult. I chose the former.

I worked hard, really hard, the first semester. As the weeks wore on, it became less and less frightening to see the admissions counselor. By the time Christmas rolled around, I was able to register for the spring classes without the probationary restriction. The whole family, especially my mother, rejoiced. I was beginning to shake off the 'zero' label. But what would I make of my life beyond college? I loved physics, mathematics, and the other exact sciences but was also occasionally drawn to the Arts side of the educational grid. I wondered if there was some way that I could combine both the Arts and the Sciences into a workable whole. I didn't know it at the time, but linguistics fit the bill. It was definitely a science but it could also be used to relate to people. I would have to wait until I got to graduate school to make that discovery.

The Boys Are Back

The Spring Break crowd was growing larger and more unruly as it gathered on the Ft. Lauderdale beach. Caught in the middle and unsure which direction I should turn in, I suddenly felt the painful sting of the police baton whacked across my right knee. "Keep moving to your left!" was the command. Five of us plus Cory had joined the annual trek south but this was not my idea of fun. It was March 1970.

I got to know Cory that semester and we decided to go to Chicago in order to look for summer work. Rumor had it that certain trucking companies were looking for summer help and in response, my brother and I decided to make an initial trip to the Windy City to look for employment. A glance at the "I-Need-A-Ride" bulletin board in the college dining hall told us that a girl named Penny was looking for a ride in the same direction. Cory promised us that if we weren't successful in Chicago that weekend, we could ride with him two weeks later to continue the search.

Penny and my brother and I, piled into Cory's brand new Malibu for the three-hour drive to Illinois and soon discovered that Penny was a missionary kid (MK) whose parents were serving in Papua New Guinea. I remember thinking how ridiculous it was to have one's parents on the other side of the world while you were going to school in Michigan. We didn't talk much about it on our short sojourn that May afternoon but it did strike me, nonetheless, as being quite odd. When we pulled up to the house to drop Penny off, a woman in her early 50s wearing a flowered kitchen apron ran out of the house, arms raised, a huge smile on her face. "Oh, Penny! It is so good to see you," she exclaimed, "We have been praying for you and your family and it's wonderful to finally have you here with us!" Penny's face lit up and it was obviously clear that she felt immediately at home. We understood that Penny would be staying for a few days and then head out to the west coast to catch a flight for Papua New Guinea and spend the summer with her parents who were serving as Bible translators in that far-flung land.

The woman with the flowered apron was Mrs. Kallemeyn. When she heard that we were in town looking for summer work she said, "If you're not successful this time around, please come back another time and consider staying with us." The invitation seemed incredible from someone we had only met a few minutes earlier.

We spent a frustrating day in south Chicago. Every trucking company we approached assured us they had all the employees they needed. We didn't have any union cards and we had no further leads. When the day was over we headed back to Michigan, our heads slung low, our energy depleted. Maybe those jobs in Chicago didn't really exist and we were just chasing false leads. We promised ourselves, however, that we would give it one more try the following week. And with Cory and his newer car, we'd have a better chance of not breaking down in our ailing Ford Falcon.

Cory said that he would be ready to go to Chicago again the following week. The week dragged by. On Friday morning, we waited for Cory to show up. We waited and waited but no Cory. Had he slept in? Had he forgotten? We would never find out. By three o'clock we had given up on seeing him. Angrily, I got into our vehicle, convinced it would surely break down on the way to Chicago. I was still fuming when my brother shoved the car into first gear and drove off. I complained all the way to Chicago. My disappointment didn't go unnoticed by my brother. He took it all in stride, convinced that Someone else knew what our needs were. Where would we go?

We didn't have much of a plan and decided to go back to the only person we knew, Mrs. Kallemeyn. No sooner had we pulled into the driveway three hours later when she came running out of the house, bounding down the short outdoor stairs, arms flung out wide open, crying, "The boys are back! The boys are back!" Who was this woman, we asked, and why was she so intent on greeting us like we were her own children? "Oh, you must have supper with us and spend the night," she said, as she started to prepare dinner for her family. The spacious kitchen and equally large kitchen table looked like it could seat more than a dozen people. Over tea she told us that she and her husband had ten children, and having two more around the house wouldn't be much of an issue. We grabbed our few belongings and put them into a small spare basement bedroom of the large two-story house. At suppertime we were introduced to her husband and eight of their ten children. He asked us if we had been successful in finding work and when we replied that we hadn't, he suggested we apply at the Ford factory, a few miles away. "Go down to their employment office," he said, "and fill in a new application each day you go there."

That evening around the dinner table we were introduced to an amazing family. They had one son named David. We quickly became friends. After dinner Dave started to tell me about a course he had taken in North Dakota the summer before. It was focused on languages and linguistics. I was hardly listening but distinctly remember thinking, "What is the difference between those two?" The answer would have a huge impact on me.

In the morning we headed to the Ford factory and filled in applications. The following morning we repeated our actions. By the time Friday rolled around, we had applied five times. The employment officer called us over and told us to report for work the following Monday afternoon. Good advice and persistence had paid off. We both received assembly line jobs, making more money than ever before. It was 1970 and the hourly wage was $4.08 an hour.

After three weeks of living with the Kallemeyns, they offered us a small unoccupied house that was located right next to their printing operation. We gladly moved in and set up house. We were also offered part-time jobs at the printing press which supplemented our income. At the Ford Motor Company, my brother ended up in the paint department and I started in the door assembly area, installing door lock buttons and window cranks on the new Ford Galaxy. I made a few friends on the floor but one in particular stood out. He had attended Moody Bible Institute and I was immediately drawn to him. I had only recently heard about Moody but it didn't interest me a lot at the time. My life would take a drastic turn, though, in the coming weeks. It wasn't until many years later that I realized that going to Florida with Cory, and his not showing up to take us to Chicago that Friday afternoon, had all been

55

carefully crafted and planned by an unseen hand. God was quietly and firmly in control, doing what He does best. A masterpiece was in the making and I was part of it, little knowing what lay in store for me.

Lord, Please Change Me

"Hey Ed," Dave called out, "do you want to go to the Loop with us to the Moody Church?" I declined citing a previous engagement, although my reason was weak at best. I had gone to church all my life and had read the Bible on a daily basis for many years. How could the Moody Church improve on that? I had other 'more important' issues that evening. I would visit some friends, have a few beers and listen to Led Zeppelin, Iron Butterfly, and other heavy metal groups of the early 70s. I was determined to have a good time that warm and muggy Friday evening in June 1970.

My friends were waiting for me. The impossible lyrics of Jimi Hendrix, the screaming, gravelly voice of Janis Joplin, and the heavy bass of Iron Butterfly would be our friends this evening. The windows were already rattling in response. We swapped albums and after a few hours and a couple of beers, I made my way back to the house where we were staying that summer.

No sooner had I arrived when Dave and my brother walked into the bedroom. He was carrying a cassette tape. "What's that?' I inquired. "It's a recording of tonight's message," he said, tossing it onto the bed. "There's a player here if you want to listen to it."

I popped the cassette into the player. "What harm can it do?" I thought. "At least I didn't have to drive all the way to downtown Chicago to hear this guy." From the moment the tape started playing, I was completely engrossed in the message. This guy talked my language. It was mesmerizing. He understood the current culture and knew how to communicate. I was about two-thirds of the way through the one-hour message when the evangelist quoted a verse from the book of Philippians. Chapter 4 verse 8, *"Finally, brethren, whatever is true, whatever is honorable, whatever is just, whatever is pure, whatever is lovely, whatever is gracious, if there is any excellence, if there is anything worthy of praise, think about these things."*

I stopped the recorder in mid-sentence. My mind went back in a quick review of my life. I was twenty years old, and realized that I had somehow missed the mark. As the tape of my life rolled out before me, I asked myself what in my life was true, honorable, just, pure, gracious, or lovely. Hardly anything, I concluded. How could I have been so blind? Why hadn't I seen this before? I started to sob like a blubbering baby. And I couldn't stop. Through my tears I could see the newly acquired LPs lying on the bed. Deep down, I knew that this kind of music was not helping me in my search for God. The lyrics alone were proof enough. I picked up the albums, and to my brother's astonishment, smashed them to pieces over my knee. Still sobbing uncontrollably, I got on my knees beside my bed and prayed a really simple, short prayer. "Lord," I said, "I accept your forgiveness. Please change me."

The sobbing subsided but something had happened, something marvelous. I couldn't describe it but something wonderful had just taken place. I went to bed and slept like a log. In the morning I picked up my Bible and started to read. As I read, I couldn't believe that these were the same words I had read so many times. Was this really the Bible? I turned it over. Sure enough, it said "Holy Bible." How could it be so different from one day to the next? Someone must have rewritten it. I knew that was impossible. No, the Bible hadn't changed but I had. Scales had fallen from my eyes and I was reading it through a different lens.

Years later, I argued with myself that I hadn't said the 'right words' in giving my life to Christ that evening. I struggled with this but came to the grateful conclusion that it was not in the words but rather in the attitude of my heart and the prominent change in my lifestyle that had become apparent to me and others. I saw Christ in a new light, His light. It wasn't the prayer that saved me, but the realization I had come to that I couldn't possibly save myself. I was doomed and I knew it. There was no way out.

That knowledge propelled me to take a stance that I have never regretted. I can't explain the mechanics of what took place that evening but I can testify to the profound change that overtook me. It was not any doing of my own but rather, I was responding to the Holy Spirit's tug on my life.

Over the next few days I devoured the Scriptures. They were alive with meaning and purpose. I read and re-read the exact same passages I had read as a child. They started to make sense. Jesus' words and deeds as recorded in the Gospels rang with truth and clarity. I couldn't get enough. Every chance I had I opened my Bible and lost myself in the fabulous words. Words of truth, words of grace, words of honor, and best of all, words of love. I cried as I read, and I shared the words with others around me. Jesus had spoken directly to my wayward heart, and I responded with thanksgiving and humility. I understood now that this was the reason for my mother's daily rejoicing. I was a new man but there would be some serious testing in store for me.

In August I returned to college for my sophomore year and immediately enrolled in two campus Bible studies. I was flying high. As I dug into God's Word, it started to take on a life of its own. Passages made sense. I discovered nuggets of gold, and I wanted to share them with others. On the way to the college library one evening, I was viciously attacked by an inner-city youth wielding a leather whip. I tried to avoid him by crossing the street, but he followed me and hit me with his four-foot truncheon. I ran as fast as I could to a friend's house who quickly helped soothe my welts. I had thoughts of retribution but quickly put them aside. Something was different.

In the spring of 1971 I went with a group of college students to Florida for Spring Break, not to party and get drunk but to do beach evangelism. I had tried the former a couple of years earlier but it brought no satisfaction. Trying the latter and seeing complete strangers give their lives to God while standing in the Ft. Lauderdale surf made much more sense.

Dave, who had suggested I attend the Moody Church and who knew I was good with languages, gave me a pamphlet that touched on the topic of Bible translation and linguistics. I glanced at the literature but promptly put the idea out of my mind. Didn't linguistics have something to do with how many languages a person spoke? At the time I didn't realize what the difference was.

That fall I looked into the possibility of spending Christmas and New Year's in the Mexican border town of Ciudad Juarez, across the river from El Paso, Texas. Operation Mobilization (O.M.) made an annual trek to this populous region to distribute literature and get a feel for short term trips. I signed up at the urging of my friend Harry. He had been on the same trip several years earlier and made a suggestion that would dramatically change the course of my thinking. "When you get to El Paso," he said, "you're going to be brought to a church. At the end of the meeting, the leader is going to voluntarily divide you into two groups. One group will stay on the U.S. side and the rest will go to the Mexican side. Make sure you choose for the Mexican side because you'll learn a lot that way. It will be far more exciting."

"But Harry," I stammered, "I don't know any Spanish." "Well, then this will be a great opportunity to learn, won't it?" he returned. I had to agree and when the moment arrived, I raised my hand for the Mexican experience. I never regretted that decision and later thanked Harry profusely.

For a solid week I was immersed into the Mexican culture, food, and language. We walked the streets of Juarez, handing out leaflets and pamphlets, inviting people to the nightly church services. One afternoon, a colleague and I led a young eight-year-old boy to make a decision for Christ. The young boy nodded in agreement when we asked him if he wanted to believe in Jesus. He was about to pray with us on that crowded sidewalk when a strong hand landed on his shoulder. His father grabbed him and pulled him away, muttering something about foreigners this and foreigners that. The young boy glanced back at us, nodding. Off he went.

Partway through the week, George Verwer, the founder of O.M., arrived in Juarez. That evening he briefly addressed our little group. "This is no time for spiritual goose bumps," he said, "and this is no time for spiritual platitudes. God is in our midst, and he has something he wants to accomplish in your lives. Don't miss out on the opportunities afforded you this week." George immediately launched into a prayer that would stick with me the rest of my life. This man meant business and had no time for superficial talk.

That short week in Juarez culminated with a combined service in the church we were staying in. The others who had chosen to stay north of the border crossed the river and joined us for a final celebration. Partway through the service, the pastor looked at me and asked me if I wanted to sing a song for the gathering. I was dumbstruck. Why me? Apparently it was assumed that one of the foreigners would sing during the service and he picked me out of the crowd. Regrettably, I turned down his request, much to everyone's dismay. Many years later, while sitting in a large gathering during a three-week trip to a remote part of the Philippines, the pastor looked at me and invited me to come up to the stage to sing a hymn. I jumped out of my seat, remembering the mistake I had made 30 years earlier. Visions of my mother singing her Psalms danced in my head as I sang.

The Ontario Angel

The grinding, shrieking sound from the front axle confirmed my suspicion. The wheel bearing had failed and welded itself onto the axle on the right side of the car. We came to a screeching halt in no man's land, a potential nightmare in the making. That Sunday evening in the summer of 1972 found us standing on the side of Highway 401 in southern Ontario, staring at the wheel of the now-immobilized car. Dallas seemed an unfathomable long ways off. We were traveling to Texas to attend Explo '72, but this was not a good beginning. Our faith was definitely being challenged.

Traffic was sparse that Sunday evening. Few cars passed us as we stood on the side of the road. What chance was there that someone would stop to assist us? Cell phones were still a distant dream; the nearest exit miles away. The lonely farmhouse, about a mile away, didn't show any signs of life. The only tool we had at our disposal was prayer. Our quartet huddled in the car and took turns praying for God to be glorified in this seemingly hopeless situation. We prayed, nonetheless, believing that He had heard our request.

Ten minutes went by, then twenty, then thirty. A white truck pulled up, headlights blinding us. Two men got out and walked over to our stranded vehicle. "How may we help you?" one asked. When we told him our problem, they climbed back into their vehicle, and promised to be back shortly. We didn't know whether to believe them or not, but we had no other choice. We settled back into the car, wondering what the Lord had in store for us. Surely there was no car dealership open on a late Sunday evening. Car parts stores, likewise, would have closed their doors hours ago even if they had been open on Sunday. With nothing else to do but pray and wait, we once again committed the whole affair to the Lord's guidance.

I remember an incident that happened many years later in Suriname, when I heard the Lord speaking directly to me. I was driving behind a panel truck, attempting to pass the big box-like vehicle. It was a sweeping blind curve. As I pulled out to pass, I heard a voice out of nowhere say, "No. Don't!" Obediently I swerved back behind the panel truck. Within seconds a car appeared from behind the yellow truck, racing the other way. The Lord had spared me from an ugly accident. I was more than a little bit thankful to have heard His voice. An angel?

Meanwhile, back in Ontario and another thirty minutes later, the white truck once again pulled up behind us. This time the glaring headlights were a welcome sight. The two men were dressed like construction workers. There were no markings on the side of their vehicle, making their identification impossible. They jacked up the front wheel, removed the tire and started hammering on the bearing that had welded itself to the spindle. Within minutes, they installed a new wheel bearing and put the wheel back on. Our vehicle was repaired and we were free to go. We asked the men who they were but they declined to tell us. We asked them who they worked for but no answers were forthcoming. We asked them how we could repay them for their generosity but they said, "Just put in a good word for us if you come across any stranded motorists." They would accept payment for neither their services nor the parts. How was this possible?

Over the next few years we attempted to find out if some roving band of car mechanics roamed the Ontario highway system, looking for marooned motorists. We came to the conclusion that God had sent two angels that evening, dressed as construction workers to carry out his will. In the future I would never doubt the presence of angels, doing the Lord's bidding.

Are You Sure?

"Are you sure you know what you're doing? You won't be graduating with your class if you drop out of school now." The lady behind the desk in the Finance Office looked at me with pity and puzzlement. I had one semester left before I could graduate from college but I had run out of money. With a last ditch effort, I approached her to plead my case. The notice said that I wouldn't be allowed to register for my final semester unless I made an initial payment for the classes. Now I stood in the office, notice in hand, asking if they had any more options for me.

The lady said, "OK. I think we can help you. Why don't you take out a loan and then you can walk with your class in May."

"But madam, I'm not comfortable taking out a loan for anything, even tuition. I would rather get out of school, get a job and save up the money and then come back in the fall and finish in December," I explained. "Do you think there might be some grant or scholarship funds available somewhere?" She pointed to the office across the hallway, "You'll have to go across the hall and talk to the people over there. Perhaps they can help you." As I turned to go, I could just hear her talking to her colleagues. The softly spoken words spilled over the glass barrier, but they were unmistakable and included words like 'poor boy, doesn't want a loan, won't graduate, May, December, stubborn,' and others. I was determined not to take out a loan. I would work hard for the next eight months, register for my final semester of classes and finish in December.

I walked across the hallway and asked to see the person in charge of determining grants and scholarships. When I explained my situation the gentleman asked me, "Are you sure you want to drop out now? You might not finish, you know? Most people that drop out never return. Why don't you take out a loan and finish with your class in May?" I reassured him that I would finish.

As I walked out of the second office, I thought of everything that had happened during the last three-and-half years. When I came to college, I found myself in the admissions office without a hope or a prayer of even getting to the first class. Three-and-a-half years later I stood on the verge of graduation. The exit sign seemed a bit far away, however, I was confident that I would finish and finish well.

During the last couple of years I had involved myself with an off-campus ministry that specialized in Bible memorization and Bible studies. I had met my wife Linda at one of those Bible studies. I seriously wanted to date this gal, but Alfred, the Bible study leader, did his best to help us men stay focused on the ministry, not the girls. On a particular weekend, he had made the decision that we needn't be at his house for the weekly meeting. It was a free weekend. Another friend, Don, was interested in one of the other girls in the study, and together we decided to ask them out. When the word got out that Don and Ed were going out on a double date, Alfred quietly called us over and said we were needed at his house for some yard work. I wondered when I was ever going to get the chance to spend some extended time with Linda. Something was going to have to change, but what?

I went back to my job, working as many hours as I could. The cash started to pile up, and by the time fall registration rolled around, I had enough money to pay for the classes plus room and board. I had stayed in the ministry during the spring and Alfred invited me to come and live with him and his wife at their house for my last semester. I turned it down. We met over coffee when he said, "If you're not willing to come to our house, then you're not willing to become a man of God!" I stared in disbelief, tears welling up in my eyes. But I stood my ground. It was the last time I would see Alfred.

I hit the books, this time taking classes I had wanted to take earlier. The idea of doing mission work also appealed to me but I didn't find even one class labeled 'Missions' in the course catalog. Instead, I ended up taking a class in Ethics. This seemed like a reasonable choice. My newfound faith dealt a lot with ethics and this would be a good option. About three weeks into the semester, a student asked a question, the answer to which rocked my world. She asked, "How does God fit into all of this discussion?" The professor shot back, "We don't talk about God in this class!" I was stunned, as were many other students. We were in a Christian institution of higher learning and we can't talk about God? To this day, I haven't been able to figure out if the prof said it to provoke the students or if it was meant in truth. In any case, we all stupidly remained silent, not wanting to challenge the instructor or incur his wrath. I couldn't wait to graduate.

In the meantime, I heard about a prayer group that was starting up. My friend Dave had alerted me to it and when I arrived, I knew they meant business with God. I walked into the meeting with maps spread across the large braided rug on the living room floor, highlighting the areas where missionaries were working. Colorful newsletters and prayer cards were scattered everywhere. A group of serious students from several colleges gathered that evening. We prayed about every concern expressed. Not a single prayer request was left unaddressed.

It was ten o'clock by the time the first round of prayer was over. Snacks and coffee were served and within 15 minutes, we were once again on our knees, petitioning God on behalf of those serving overseas. At midnight we took another 15 minute break, and then went into round 3. No one moved and no one left. By the time four o'clock rolled around, we had prayed through every request several times. I walked back to my apartment in those early morning hours, feeling as if I had really done business with God. I felt invigorated and couldn't wait for next week Friday evening. Week after week I attended the prayer meeting, feeling more and more connected with the group and with those serving overseas. What would it be like, I questioned, to be one of those missionaries living and serving in another country?

In my sophomore year I had pulled an all-nighter in an attempt to get a research paper done. I felt so miserable the following day that I decided that it would be the first and last all-nighter I would ever experience. But staying up all night on Friday evenings, praying for God's work and God's people, had the opposite effect on me. I felt immensely energized and invigorated. There was a sense that the group had accomplished something worthwhile. Storming the gates of heaven took on new meaning. The only drawback was that it was all too quickly coming to a halt. I would graduate in December, head back home to an uncertain future, and to parents that were experiencing marital problems. Would I survive?

Propellers and Bibles

It was January 1974. I was standing in a deep snowdrift, looking for the 2 x 4s buried beneath the growing mound of heavy wet flakes. Just a month before, I had graduated from college and found my way back home to a job in residential construction in London, Ontario. The old farmhouse was still standing, but there were rumors that the 600 acres the house was sitting on might be up for sale. If that was the case, then it would be razed and the acreage turned into a housing development. In the meantime, I settled into the familiar routine of getting up before dawn each morning and going to my day job. Swinging a hammer had become second nature but working outdoors in the winter would be a new experience. Each morning I dressed for working in freezing or below freezing temperatures. When the weather was such that we couldn't work outdoors, we looked for indoor work, which wasn't always easy to find.

Getting up early also meant that I could spend time reading my Bible and in prayer before heading out into the cold. Alfred's words about my not wanting to be 'a man of God' had put some fear into me. Could I survive not having 'those specific ministry partners' around me? I quickly discovered that the spiritual disciplines I had learned in the preceding years would stand me in good stead. I was arming myself for the inevitable onslaught I would experience working in construction. Crude jokes and coarse language were the staples of this working world. I had acquired a pocket New Testament and it quickly became my friend during coffee and lunch breaks. I was never dubbed a holy roller but felt the stares from my fellow employees, nonetheless.

When the lunch truck rolled around to the work sites, men eagerly lined up to buy coffee, donuts, and other offerings. It was easy to see how an hour's wage could be gone in a matter of seconds, succumbing to the aroma drifting from the maggot wagon, as it was affectionately dubbed. Every evening I prepared sandwiches and break food to take with me the following morning, saving me precious dollars. My mission was clear: stay out of debt, pile up cash, and prepare for graduate school. I didn't have the slightest clue how that would unfold, but I knew that I would not be long in the construction world. God had something different in store for me.

As the daylight hours steadily increased and winter gave way to milder temperatures and the thaw of spring, I received a newsletter that would give further direction to my life. I was invited to join a group that would spend nine weeks in Mexico for the summer. Four weeks would be spent at a Spanish language school in Puebla, then a week at Jungle Camp, located in the state of Chiapas near the Guatemalan border. For the final four weeks we would live with a missionary somewhere in Mexico, using any skills we had acquired in service to the missionary family. It all sounded quite intriguing, and I quietly wondered if perhaps this is what I had been looking for but had failed to find while in college.

I applied and was accepted to the program. I gulped, took a deep breath, and showed the acceptance letter to my Dad and Mom. Dad seemed disinterested and distant, with other things on his mind. Occasional comments could be heard to indicate that there was continuous trouble brewing in my parents' marriage. Mom, however, made it a point to pray about the letter with me and together we committed it to the Lord for His direction. As the time approached I felt the excitement building. I contacted our local church about it, and they in turn committed to partially fund the experience. I was incredibly grateful for their interest and readiness to assist me.

The literature said that we would be spending a few days at the Mexico headquarters of the Summer Institute of Linguistics (SIL), a sister organization of Wycliffe Bible Translators. The week of Jungle Camp would be spent at a facility operated by SIL. I didn't know what it all meant but it didn't really matter. I sensed, however, that God was directing my steps. I moved ahead cautiously. When I joined the group in June, I discovered there were some 30 participants. My employer had graciously given me time off with the assurance that my job would still be available in late August. I was ready for a new adventure.

The four weeks of Spanish language school in Puebla were vastly different from any type of other language study I had ever encountered. In high school I had studied French and Latin, and in college I improved my boyhood Dutch. Living in a Spanish-speaking environment 24 hours a days, 7 days a week, almost guaranteed success in learning this Romance language. 'La comida esta muy sabrosa', would be a phrase I would use frequently. Indeed, Mexican food was exceptionally tasty. My palate had sent me the signal that food from other parts of the world would easily agree with me. By the time the one week Jungle Camp experience rolled around, I was as ready as I had ever been for the excitement that was just around the corner.

The bus trip up to San Cristobal de las Casas was as extreme as I had ever experienced. Hundreds of ornate shrines lined the twisting road, reminders that the hairpin curves through this mountainous terrain had taken their toll on fellow travelers. There were precious few guardrails in this part of the world and the rusting carcasses of buses and cars were clearly visible in the deep gorges and valleys. It was scary and thrilling, all at the same time. In just three hours our Cristobal Colon highway bus would climb east from Tuxtla Gutierrez (elevation 1700 feet) to Las Casas (elevation 7000 feet), a town that was frequented by more than seven different indigenous language groups. I was beginning to understand why my heart was bursting inside of me. A steady and colorful parade of ethnic peoples made their way through the town's narrow cobblestone streets. Loads were transported on people's heads or backs. Tumplines were everywhere. Firewood, fruit, vegetables, sugarcane, furniture; whatever needed to be transported could be done using the centuries old technique of the tumpline. I tried not to stare but it was impossible. I had taken a professional photography course just a few weeks earlier, and my SLR clicked away employing my newly acquired skills. The colorful markets, the Cathedral, the narrow alleyways, and the babble of the different languages consumed me. My mind had a difficult time taking in the cornucopia of sights, sounds, and smells but I relished every minute of it. Little did I know though, that I would be in for the ride of my life, just a day away.

Early the next morning we drove to Ocosingo, and on the edge of town we gathered at an airstrip. Two small single-engine planes, both of them Cessna 185s operated by Mission Aviation Fellowship (MAF) with cargo pods slung beneath their bellies, were ready to take us on the last leg of our journey into the wilds of southern Chiapas to Jungle Camp. I waited my turn to be transported over the thick canopy of tall jungle trees, which pushed their leafy branches skyward in search of sunlight. It would take several trips to transport our group of thirty to Yaxoquintela, the site of Jungle Camp. The small craft were capable of carrying only five passengers and some cargo. It would be my first experience in an aircraft this small and countless thoughts raced through my head as I tried to grasp the significance of the moment. As we strapped ourselves in and the powerful engine roared to life, I had no idea how the next twelve minutes would impact me. I was fortunate to sit in the front seat next to the pilot, wearing a pair of headphones.

We bounced down the little airstrip, gaining speed. I looked over my shoulder at the others. Unlike me, some were clearly not enjoying this part of the experience. We had almost reached the end of the undulating sloping gravel and grass airstrip, when the pilot pulled back on the yoke. The airplane rotated and we were airborne. My heart jumped into my throat. This was flying and here you could experience what it was meant to be like. Every updraft or downdraft was felt. The treetops seemed to be within one's grasp. Small communities dotted the landscape below. The engine's deep roar echoed off the steep canyon walls. My excitement rose to fever pitch. As a youngster, my Dad would take me to the local airport in London, just to watch the DC-3s and DC-6s take off and land. I longed to travel by air but the little flying I had done had all been on commercial aircraft. This jungle flying was vastly different and far more thrilling.

All too quickly the little Cessna started its descent. We could clearly see the camp below us, the narrow river twisting around the far end. The young pilot made a hard left turn and banked and we observed people on the ground making their way to the short grassy airstrip. The pilot made a final adjustment, lowered the flaps and lined up his approach. The stall horn sounded and we were on the ground. Just like that, it was over. Twelve minutes ago we had been standing on the ground in Ocosingo. Twelve minutes later we were on the ground in Yaxoquintela.

The plane disgorged its anxious occupants and precious cargo. I stood there in awe and fascination. Why did we have to take an airplane into Jungle Camp? Why didn't we take the road? I had seen various roads as we descended those several thousand feet to the camp. It quickly dawned on me that the same short distance would have taken us many tortuous hours to traverse. If the rivers were swollen, some of the roads would be impassable. If a small bridge was out because of high water, the journey would have been impossible. I was starting to see the logic of mission aviation. It was a time saver; it afforded the passenger the opportunity to arrive refreshed and ready to work. Hours, if not days, could be shaved off the time to reach one's destination.

I had a lot of questions for that pilot, and I prayed that I would have the opportunity to ask them. Is this what God had in store for me? Was I meant to be a missionary pilot? If so, how does one begin? I was 24 years old, and the pilots didn't seem much older than me. I would have to get started in my training right away. As we walked the short distance to the dining hall, I heard the Cessna's engine roar back to life. The pilot had swung the plane around to pick up his next load from Ocosingo. As it leapt into the air, I turned to watch. This time the high-winged plane lifted off with ease having shed its heavy burden. The sight and the sound of it would become permanently etched in my memory.

Whenever I hear the unmistakable whine of a small airplane, I crane my neck heavenward to catch a glimpse of the aircraft. Often I pray for those in the far-flung places of the world. I always associate it with the beginning of a new dream and vision. My excitement continued to rise as we settled into Jungle Camp, the place that would become our home for one week. I was already eagerly anticipating the return flight to Ocosingo, seven days away. I was on a mission and had some serious questions to ask. The possibility of becoming a missionary pilot took on real meaning. I had not expected this to be one of the outcomes of going to Mexico the summer of 1974 but something was tugging at my heart.

The week at Jungle Camp passed by quickly. We learned how to live in an environment that had none of the standard luxuries that most people back home deem as necessities. Running water, electricity, paved roads, flush toilets, sewers, grocery stores a short distance away…you name it; none of that was within reach now. It had all been stripped away. And it was intentional. Anyone who dreamed of becoming a missionary in the developing world would probably have to learn how to do without some of these luxuries, and Jungle Camp was the classroom.

Added to the mix was the Tzeltal language spoken in this part of southern Mexico, a stone's throw from the Guatemalan border. Thousands of Tzeltals had become believers since the Scriptures were translated here by two single women working with SIL. The result of their work was the completion of the New Testament in Tzeltal and dozens upon dozens of churches that had sprung up in this valley. People had been trained in the use of the Scriptures, as there was a Bible school not far away in another valley.

When our assignments for the last four weeks were announced, I was flying high. I would stay in Tzeltal country but move to a different valley. That meant I would fly in MAF's Cessna 185 to Buenos Aires, a village about 20 minutes away. My assignment would include helping the missionary finish the construction of a literacy center. I could already see how God was using all of my background to accomplish His will in my life.

When the time came to leave Yaxoquintela to take the short flight to Buenos Aires (Mexico) along with Darryl, my partner for the next few weeks, the confidence that missionary work would become my life was almost assured. I flew out of Jungle Camp, not realizing that in four short years, I would be back to this exact spot. But the circumstances under which I would come would be markedly different.

How Do I Get There?

A s the Cessna lined up for its approach into the village of Buenos Aires, we saw that the wide grass strip was dotted with black forms. "Cattle," the pilot said over the intercom. "We'll have to buzz the strip before we can land." Ross pointed the nose of the aircraft down, revved up the engine and made a low swooping pass over the grazing and unsuspecting cows. Within seconds they were scurrying to the edge of the strip, out of harm's way. He pulled the nose up, and we made a wide sweeping 360 degree turn. The mission station was now in clear view. A rather large house was at the top of the hill, surrounded by several smaller buildings. The herd of cattle stayed to the edge of the field as we landed. The thrill of it all was starting to build with each flight. As we extricated ourselves from the airplane, Sam ran out to meet us. Sam Hoffman had been in this valley for many years, doing mission work under the auspices of the Reformed Church in America. "Helen's not here," he said, "She'll be back in a few weeks. I'll show you two to your quarters and then we can talk about your assignment." I quickly knew that we were going to get along well.

The pilot was invited to the house for some refreshment but he declined, citing his busy schedule. By now, the engine's sound had become a familiar one. As the plane escaped the bonds of gravity, it did what it was designed to do, namely, fly. The big six-cylinder's growl reverberated off the valley's hills. I couldn't helped but turn and watch it disappear over the ridge to its next destination. When would be the next time I got to fly in one of those "wings of mercy"?

Over the next several days I watched Sam closely, trying to understand what missionaries do. More importantly, I was also trying to figure out what I would need if this was to become my future. Although Spanish was the national language of Mexico, it quickly became evident that it was not always the language of choice here in this lush but rugged valley. The language spoken here was Tzeltal, a slightly different variety of the Tzeltal spoken in Jungle Camp but a close cousin. Tzeltal was preferred by the people I met. The young children and the women all spoke it, but the men could be heard speaking a mixture of Spanish and Tzeltal. Later on I would learn that the practice of using two languages interchangeably is called code switching. Certain aspects of life were talked about in one language and other aspects in a different one. It seemed whenever emotions were involved, people preferred using Tzeltal, their native tongue. A few years later I would discover the glaring truth of this principle in a whole new way. When my mother stood in that sod house in the museum, she too, had demonstrated it perfectly. She had subconsciously slipped back into the language of her childhood, the language spoken in Groningen. An important truth was working its way into my mind; if people want to understand what's going on, the communication needs to be in their native tongue.

Spanish was a latecomer to South and Central America, having arrived hundreds of years later, through the Spanish conquistadors. The Mayan languages were native to the area. They didn't look anything like this Indo-European Romance language that dominated the geography. People clung to their mother tongue because it offered them comfort and familiarity. Having the Scriptures in Tzeltal reinforced that.

"Do you want to visit some of the clinics?" Sam offered one morning over breakfast. We hopped into the open cab Jeep, strapping on our machetes as it was foolish to travel without them. The morning was spent bouncing along the 'roads', some of which were mere trails for the huge logging trucks bringing their cargo to the nearby saw mills. We stopped at one clinic after another, talking with the different workers and getting a pulse for the scope of the medical work being conducted in the valley. Everywhere we went, Tzeltal was the language of choice. Although Darryl and I were nearly always greeted in Spanish, Sam employed Tzeltal whenever he spoke. I was beginning to understand the importance of learning the local language and learning it well.

Back at the mission station in Chiapas, we set to work in the literacy center. Huge logs had been dumped off at the carpenter's shop. A sturdy rig, about six feet high, had been constructed and the heavy squared-off logs were hoisted to the top. Two Tzeltal men, one on top of the horizontal log and the other beneath, armed with a long crosscut saw, cut thin one-inch slices from the log. Their day long labor yielded several boards measuring 8 or 9 feet in length, roughly 12 inches wide.

Darryl and I were given a small hand drawn blueprint of what the literacy center should look like, complete with open shelves. We took the rough-sawn lumber and constructed the shelving to display the various books and booklets available in the Tzeltal language, the sum total of which easily fit into the building now dubbed The Literacy Center. For the better part of four weeks, we worked the design to reflect the hand drawn plan. On his periodic visits to the literacy center, Sam would nod in agreement or give further suggestions.

As I observed Sam, I realized that what was happening in this valley was of great importance and significance. Because the language had been preserved, the culture likewise, was being preserved. Because the Scriptures were translated into Tzeltal, the church was growing in the communities in the highlands of Chiapas. Everywhere we went, small churches had sprung up and people gathered on a frequent basis to worship God in their own language. The picture forming in my mind was becoming clearer by the day. Learn the language, help people translate the Scriptures into the language, and you'll be engaging in building God's Kingdom. But then questions started to form in my mind. How do I get there? What do I need to do to see that happen somewhere? And what about this mission aviation idea? How does that fit into the puzzle? Could I perhaps do both? One thing was certain. I was going to have to get some further training, either in aviation, Bible translation, or both.

Shattered Dreams

As the four weeks at the mission station unfolded, the thought of doing mission work took a serious hold on me. Was there a way that my language abilities could be used for Kingdom causes? Watching Sam move about the Tzeltal community made me realize that being able to communicate in the language that the locals speak might be one of the best tools that could be employed while working in a cross-cultural, cross-lingual environment. Sam, meanwhile, made it clear that he and others were heavily engaged in the translation of the Tzeltal Old Testament.

We visited village after village, attending worship services in the small churches that were sprouting up like mushrooms in the lush valleys. None of the churches were large, averaging 40 to 80 people, but they were thriving. That was intriguing. The scenario was the same, no matter which church or which village we visited. The Tzeltals were usually standing outside their treasured churches just prior to the start of the service. Men were talking to men and women to women. Children darted between the adults.

As they entered, men went to sit on one side of the church and women on the other. Young children sat with their mothers, but older boys sat with the fathers and girls with their mothers. Some nursed babies. The women had long black hair braided with colorful ribbons. Their embroidered tops were stunningly beautiful and worn with floor length skirts garlanded with ribbons and embroidered patterns. The small churches were awash with vivid colors. The men usually wore light colored pants, with white shirts and sombreros.

There was no mistaking we were in Mexico. With the unique seating arrangement, it was a challenge trying to figure out who was married to whom. Years later, in Suriname, Linda and I would often be stymied by this same issue. It would be months or even years before we determined who was married to whom. It seemed the method we employed back in North America with the husband and wife sitting together in church, was a cultural tradition, not a Biblical one. I reasoned that getting some training in cultural anthropology was a given.

But more was needed before one could begin work in a language group that had no written language. Marianna Slocum and Florence Gerdel, two single missionaries, had completed the translation of the Tzeltal New Testament in 1956, a project that took some 15 years to complete. How did they do that if the language didn't even have an alphabet? This had been an oral culture only, back in the 1940s when the two young women arrived to begin their work. I had to get some answers, and Sam would be the one to supply them.

I could hardly wait for suppertime. "Sam," I started, "I've been observing you these past two weeks. The idea of doing Bible translation is starting to fascinate me. What kind of training is needed?"

"You would have to get some linguistic training," he said.

"I've studied a number of languages already," I told him, "but there was nothing in those courses that even comes close to what you and others have accomplished here. What else is needed?"

"Linguistic training will help you discover how a language is put together. It won't teach you the language, as is done in high school or college, but it will provide you with the tools to unlock the secrets of the inner workings of a language: its sound system, its grammar, how to establish an alphabet, and how to go about learning to speak a previously unwritten language." I was totally engrossed in the conversation.

"Where do you get this kind of training?"

"There's a school in Dallas called the Summer Institute of Linguistics that specializes in this training. I attended the SIL school in Oklahoma a few years ago. It's now located in south Dallas near Duncanville. I'll get you some contact information," he offered.

The wheels were starting to spin faster and faster and I was inching closer to the answers I was looking for. The leaders of this nine-week summer training session, Dick (Dr. Van) and Thea Van Halsema, had carefully crafted the program to include four weeks with local missionaries and their efforts were being rewarded richly. Just one more week remained in our Mexico experience. The literacy center was taking shape and at the end of the last week, we had the thrilling adventure of boarding the Cessna tail dragger one more time to visit the fascinating Mayan ruins in Palenque. We were privileged to go places where few tourists went. But the conflicting thoughts continued: mission aviation or linguistics and Bible translation? How do I know? And when would I find out? The answer would be forthcoming quicker than I could imagine.

We crammed ourselves into the Cessna for the final time to fly out to Tuxtla. A commercial flight to Mexico City reunited all thirty of us at SIL's headquarters in Tlalpan, one of Mexico City's southern boroughs. I needed to find the director of the SIL work and explain to him what had occurred the last few weeks; the enthusiasm and excitement I had experienced going to Jungle Camp, flying here and there with MAF, and staying with Sam in Tzeltal country. I asked him, "How does one become a missionary pilot?"

The director regarded me and asked, "Ed, how old are you?" "I'm 24, sir. Why do you ask?"

He said, "Ed, all of those pilots and others like them, all got their start in aviation when they were 15 or 16 years old. At 24 you're already too old[†] to think about getting started. It would take you years just to get ready."

Wham! It felt like being hit with a ton of bricks. Too old? I was only 24 and already too old to even think about mission aviation? My mind clouded over, and the more I thought about it, the more disappointed I became. Too old?

The two days of debriefing sped by quickly and before long I was back in London, swinging my hammer, wrestling with my conflicting thoughts. Gloom reigned. An internal struggle ensued that kept me captive for days. Just when I thought that God was clearly leading me in the direction of His choice, I was devastated. The window of

---

[†] Years later I would discover that the information I was given about being too old to go into mission aviation was incorrect. Many mission aviators started their journeys later in life. I see it now as God being in control of every situation in my life and would encourage any potential mission aviator to pursue his dream, regardless of age.

opportunity for missionary pilot training had already passed me by. God was at work behind the scenes but I wasn't privileged to see the plan. However, the time was not far away when all would become crystal clear.

The Volvo Involvement

"For Sale: Used 1968 Volvo P1800, $700"

I stared at the newspaper ad in disbelief. This was a good deal. A few days earlier I had returned from Mexico and desperately needed a car that wasn't going to leave me stranded by the side of the road, like the tired VW Squareback I had purchased during my final year in college. On my way back to school after the Thanksgiving break, the engine's head gasket had blown that left my sister and me standing by the side of the road.

I decided to give the number a try. "Yes, I still have it," the voice said on the other end, "Are you interested?" "Very much so. Could you wait until Friday until I get paid?" I returned, "I'll have the cash with me."

On Friday afternoon I cashed my paycheck, pulled most of my money out of savings, and with the $700 drove over in my sputtering VW to see the Volvo. I silently prayed that the good doctor hadn't sold the car. When I pulled into his driveway I looked for the P1800 but it wasn't there. The doctor came out of his townhouse and with a sheepish grin told me that he had just sold the car. I sighed in disappointment but before I could turn around and leave he said, "I have another Volvo here. It's a 1968, a B144S model with only 49,000 miles on it. Would you be interested in that?" "Well, I would be sir," I countered, "but it must cost substantially more, no?" When he quoted me the price tag of $2000, I knew it was far more than what I had to spend. "Thanks, but no thanks," I said. "You could always go to the bank and take out a loan," he offered, "I'll hold the car for you. Go talk to your bank and see if they'll loan you the money."

Now my mind was spinning. I had never borrowed money. To be taking out a $1300 loan was beyond my imagination. How do people live with themselves, I thought, when they owe other people money? In college, I had memorized Romans 13:8 that read "Owe nothing to anyone—except for your obligation to love one another. If you love your neighbor, you will fulfill the requirements of God's law." I was sure the sentence that read "Owe nothing to anyone", also applied to money.

Against everything that I believed in, I said, "OK. If you promise to hold the car for me, I'll go the bank." I turned to leave and as I did, I wheeled around to look at the navy blue car, wondering if I was making the right decision. I struggled with myself all the way to the bank. The loan officer quickly guided me into his corner office and with a stroke of the pen, held out $1300 cash, more money than I had ever seen. I cringed as I took the money and stuffed it into my pocket. Upon exiting the bank, I cautiously looked in every direction, thinking someone may have seen me leave with a wad of cash.

The next day I drove back to the seller. This time, thankfully, the blue box-like Volvo was still in the driveway. I handed over the $2000, and with a simple handshake I became the new owner of a 1968 Volvo 144S! I got in, threw the long stick into first gear, released the clutch and drove off with a heavy heart. It felt like a new car but the weight of being in debt overtook my otherwise good feelings of car ownership.

My mind wandered back to the 10th grade when Doug, a fellow student asked me for a quarter to buy some gum. I loaned it to him with his personal guarantee of repayment the next day. The next day when I asked Doug for the 25¢, he outright denied ever borrowing it from me. I had become the laughingstock of my classmates because many of them had also fallen prey to Doug's dishonesty. I promised myself that I would never loan anyone money again. I was not going to be duped. I figured that the other side of the coin looked the same; I would never borrow money either. The Scriptures were crystal clear: the borrower is slave to the lender.

All of that flashed through my head as the loan officer reminded me I had two years to pay back the loan. The interest over that period would be $68, on top of the $1300. I had always paid cash for everything and I chafed at having fallen prey to this scheme but I was stuck. I needed reliable transportation. I determined to pay it back quickly.

The weather was starting to turn and I worked as much overtime as possible. Home construction was booming and I took every outside job I could find. On a Wednesday morning, a university professor wandered onto our job site. He was looking for someone to shingle his newly framed country bungalow. On Friday afternoon, after working hard all week, I drove to the professor's new home to start the job. I worked by myself all Friday afternoon until dark and all day Saturday until sundown. By the time I hammered in the last nail on the ridge vent, it was so dark I could hardly see my hand in front of me, but the job was done and the twenty hours of work had paid me the handsome sum of $100. My satisfaction quotient shot up sky high. That $100 would go towards the car.

Over the next 6 months I quadrupled my payments and when June rolled around, I walked into the bank, and placed the last payment on the loan officer's desk. He took out my file and said, "That was quick! It only took you six months to pay off a two-year loan. What's your hurry?"

"Sir," I said, "I eschew debt. It just doesn't agree with me." Over the next months, the bank mailed me letter after letter, offering to loan me even more money for whatever I wanted. Another car? Some new clothes? How about a loan for a house? The offers kept coming but I pitched them all into the trash can. I basked in the feeling of being debt free.

The Letter from Heaven

As I settled back into the familiar routine of my day job, disturbing events were unfolding on the home front. Dad and Mom had been married for almost 30 years but things were not going well. Every now and then telling comments would be made that confirmed my suspicion.

My sister was off to college in Michigan, and in early October she called long distance to tell us that she was coming home for Canadian Thanksgiving with a few friends from her dorm floor in tow. I was still basking in the glow of having been to Mexico and anxious to share all of the stirring details with her. But it was not to be.

When she arrived late Friday evening, four girls emerged from the car: my sister, Linda, and two other friends. I had met Linda in a campus Bible study a couple of years earlier. As she walked into the kitchen, I couldn't help but notice that big, beautiful smile. Her teeth were as straight and beautiful as I had ever seen. Her dark hair had been almost waist length, but was cropped short now. She was wearing a yellow waist length ski jacket and blue jeans. Immediately I made the decision that I was going to be spending a lot of time around this girl. And that's precisely what I did, all weekend long. Every chance I had, I was next to her, practically ignoring my sister and her other friends.

As I started to tell her about my summer in Mexico, she said, "Oh, I know what you're talking about. I went on the same trip with the same organization two years ago." I couldn't believe what I was hearing. She had experienced many of the same things I had. She had been to SIL's Mexico headquarters in Tlalpan, and to Jungle Camp in Chiapas, however, the four-week assignment during the second half of the summer had taken her to Mexico City to work with a local church conducting a Vacation Bible School, among other activities. As we continued to compare notes throughout the weekend, we discovered that she loved foreign cultures, and I loved foreign languages. Her spring semester would be spent student teaching in New Mexico on an American Indian reservation. I didn't know what was next on my agenda, but more than likely it was going to include further education, somewhere. The longer we talked that weekend, the more I liked Linda. When the four girls left to drive back to college, Linda promised to write me once she arrived in New Mexico.

October lapsed into November. The weather started to turn cooler, and I was dreading the thought of spending another winter building homes in the snow and cold. I was thankful, however, for a good paying job and was saving money quickly for more schooling. In a moment, though, my world would be blown apart.

On a cold November morning, I left for work as usual. When I returned home at dusk, I drove up the driveway and knew that something was amiss. I rushed into the house and stood there stunned. I called for Mom but there was only silence. I walked through the downstairs and then the upstairs of the old farmhouse. It was as if an exact, tiny, and tidy tornado had surgically swept through the old house. Each room had been picked through carefully and half of everything was missing. In the living room, the couch was gone but the two sitting chairs were still in place. In the kitchen, half of all the dishes had been meticulously removed, as had the silverware. Upstairs, half of the beds were gone, half of the blankets and half of the pillows.

Immediately I knew that Dad had made his escape, taking exactly half of the home's contents with him. Mom would probably be at her sister's house with the news, having walked through the cornfields behind us to get there since she had never learned to drive. That's where I found her, sobbing. We looked at each other and hugged and hugged. We had each other and we determined that we would make the most of it.

We were apprehensive about going home, scared that Dad would return for the items he had overlooked. We felt defenseless. We held one another all night long. In the morning Mom went off to work, and I locked myself inside the house. At about 10 A.M., as Mom and I had predicted, Dad drove up the driveway to retrieve some items he had forgotten. I was shaking in my boots, fearing he would come into the house. He found an unlocked window, crawled in and I stood there, trembling. I yelled at him to get out, full of fear and anger. He sat down by the telephone, picked it up and told me he was going to call his lawyer. I said, "Go right ahead." The day before when he had made his exit, the moving truck had come across the front lawn and accidentally cut the phone line to the house. It was still lying, severed, in the grass. He picked up the phone but there was no dial tone. He hung it back up and walked out of the house. It would be 22 years before I would see him again, and then for the last time.

During the next few days we moved the furniture around and filled in the holes with whatever items we could find. Within a short time the house was looking lived in again, and we settled down to life without Dad. Our routine didn't change much, except that I was now spending every evening with Mom. If she needed a ride somewhere, I was available. If she went to choir practice, my trusty Volvo was ready. Grocery shopping was easily accomplished. Over the next few months our relationship deepened and soon it was the Christmas season.

When I was a child, Scrooge frequently showed up at our house during Christmas. Although Mom desperately wanted the house to be festively decorated with lights and colored ribbons, Dad would rarely join in the celebration. Somehow Mom would always find a way to wrestle a Christmas tree into the living room, but the atmosphere in our home was rarely conducive to bringing peace and joy. Any gifts that made their way under the tree were Mom's doing, as Dad chose not to participate in this 'worldly' practice. With her limited earnings, she managed to provide sweaters and other clothing that had been bought on layaway, a practice almost unheard of today.

Outdoor Christmas lights were totally absent in my adolescent years as Dad would have considered that extreme and unnecessary. But during this first winter season after Dad's hasty exit from the household, we determined that things were going to be different.

I drove Mom to choir practice one snowy Tuesday evening, raced home and got out several strings of lights that I had purchased in the previous days. There was a small pine tree, about twenty feet high that nestled right up against the front of the house. I carefully climbed onto the roof and draped several strands over the snow-covered branches, wielding the tall stepladder to complete the job. When I was done, I stepped back, made a few adjustments and pronounced it good. Mom had often dreamt of some outdoor lights and this year she was not going to be denied. An hour later I drove back to church, down the long hill of Windermere Road. I glanced back and could see the now-twinkling lights through the falling snow.

I picked Mom up, and my anticipation continued to build. My heart was beating rapidly as we drove up the hill. When we approached the driveway, Mom saw that something was different. Seeing the little tree festooned with the colorful lights, she let out a shriek and started to cry, "Oh Ed, what have you done? Oh Edward, it's so beautiful! Oh my, my, my, my, my!" Words escaped her. I stopped the car at the end of the long driveway and we both sat there for a few minutes captivated by the beautiful view. How was it possible that such a small act could have such a huge impact on our lives? Christmas 1974 is something Mom would talk about over and over again. Joy had returned to our little household.

No sooner had the Christmas tree been set up and the house completely decorated when a letter, dated December 12, 1974, arrived in the mail, a letter that I had not anticipated. I glanced at the return address and saw that it was from the director of the summer training program I had been on in the summer. I quickly ripped it open. It was an evaluation letter along with a recommendation for future service. Based on my experience that summer, the director, Dr. Van, wrote the following: *Prepare for Scripture translation and/or literacy work through linguistics and related training, to bring the Word of God to unreached peoples (adaptation to a new language and culture required).*

It was as if I had heard the voice of God. I didn't doubt it for even one second. My heart almost exploded inside of me. Was this going to be my future? I had some serious questions but the general direction I was to move in left little room for doubt. I hardly knew anything about Bible translation but I had undoubtedly seen the powerful results of it in Chiapas. How was my future education going to be funded? Who would take care of Mom if I left now to study linguistics? Mom was never one to think about her own needs and she was ecstatic at the thought of me doing Bible translation. Isn't that what she had prayed for all of her life, that all her children would follow the Lord and isn't that exactly what was happening? My siblings all found careers in teaching, public service, and nursing, serving as exclamation points to

Mom's steadfast prayers. Still, how was I to know that this was what I was meant to do?

Over the next few days I pulled the letter out and repeatedly read those astounding words. These were words of affirmation, words of direction, words of guidance, and best of all words of worth. These were not 'big zero' words. These were not 'when are you going to learn?' words. These were not words of shame or failure. Instead, these were God's words and I never regarded them otherwise. These were words that had been a long time in coming, words that I desperately wanted to hear from my father. My mother spoke these encouraging words as we children grew up but I needed to hear them from my father. And now that I had them, I would act on them immediately. Words.

In January Linda left for New Mexico to start her student teaching on a Navajo Indian reservation. Just prior to her leaving, Mom and I made a quick visit to Michigan. I wanted to see Linda one more time before she left. It would be at least five months before we would see each other again. We went for a ride in the Volvo and when we came back and sat in the driveway, I leaned over and gave her a kiss, not sure what to expect. It was a kiss neither of us would ever forget.

We were now exchanging postcards and letters. Although infrequent, these exchanges were heady and my thoughts frequently turned to imagining her in the classroom, wrestling with the bilingual situation she faced there. When a postcard finally arrived that was signed 'Love, Linda', my mind and heart raced in simultaneous excitement. Our relationship was finally going somewhere.

As the weather turned milder, I started to dream about going to Dallas to begin studying linguistics. I would catch myself singing at work while driving nails. I still wasn't totally certain if this was the route I was to follow but nothing else had turned up that was leading me in any particular direction. I knew I needed to give Bible translation a serious shot. In late May, when Linda's teaching semester in New Mexico was over, she moved back to Michigan. In a phone call, she announced that she had accepted a job for the fall and would be returning to New Mexico to teach on another Indian reservation, this time in Zuni.

No sooner had she returned to Michigan to her parent's home when I showed up on the front doorstep. The weekend trips to Michigan would become so routine that even the border guards started to recognize me. The six-hour trips one way lasted throughout the summer's warm and pleasant months. All too soon summer was over, and I prepared for the two-day trip to Dallas to start my new life as a graduate student. I thought of the guest lecturer that had spoken to my high school science class touting the perks of graduate school. Was this really happening?

Mom

On a muggy afternoon in the middle of August, I packed the Volvo with all my earthly possessions. In the morning I would set out for Dallas. As I got up the next morning, I could hear Mom's alto voice singing her Psalms. They were her constant comfort, but then it hit me. What was I doing? We had formed this great relationship over the past year-and-a-half and it felt as if I was abandoning her now. How could I possibly leave her by herself? Was I just being selfish? The doubts swirled. In the past few months Mom had never once given me any indication that I wasn't supposed to go to Dallas to return to the books. She believed I was doing what God had called me to do. Nevertheless, the troublesome doubts persisted.

As I stood on the doorstep, ready to drive down the long gravel driveway one last time, I turned to Mom and said, "I'm sorry, Mom. I can't go. I can't leave you alone like this. I feel like I'm abandoning you. Who is going to take care of you when I'm gone? Who's going to take you to church, to choir, to the hairdresser or to get you groceries? Who?" Through my tears I heard her voice, quavering but strong, "Ed, God took care of me in the Netherlands during World War I. God took care of me during World War II. God took care of me when I was left alone in Holland with you kids for that year when Dad came to Canada to get our household set up. God took care of me when we didn't have even a penny to our names. God took care of me when Dad walked out and God will take care of me again, right here, right now. If you don't go to Dallas to start your studies to become a Bible translator, you will be disobedient to God. Burn your bed. God will take care of me."

Now we were both in tears, hugging and kissing. I got into the car, drove down the driveway, looked into the rear-view mirror and saw her standing there, waving and praying. I cried all the way to Clarksville, Tennessee, a 10-hour drive. And the next day I cried all the way to Dallas, Texas, another 10-hour drive. I was not prepared for the searing Dallas heat of late August. My Volvo didn't have air-conditioning. That was considered a luxury back in 1975. But I was here. Thankfully the dorms had air and I quickly settled into my classes. The excitement had begun.

BURN YOUR BED

Sam Was Right

In less than a week it dawned on me that studying linguistics was like hitting the jackpot. The material was revolutionary. It satisfied a deep, unrealized, personal need, to know how language functioned. I had studied classroom Latin, French, and Spanish but to learn *how* these languages operated awakened a deep longing. It also helped me to understand why people had difficulty speaking or learning another language. In our mono-cultural, monolingual society we were rarely exposed to other languages. We didn't hear people speak them, so we rarely developed an ear for them. That is not the case in multilingual societies.

The course in phonetics was a magnificent revelation to me. By understanding the inner workings of the human speech mechanism, I learned that any speech sound in any language could be reproduced. What is typically called 'an accent' is usually caused by the position of one's tongue or how one breathes. It was fascinating.

The courses dovetailed with each other and before long, I knew that Sam was right: studying linguistics was the key to becoming a future Bible translator. If I was going to work in an unwritten language somewhere, then I would need the tools that were available through linguistics. Within three short months, I decided to apply for membership to the Wycliffe Bible Translators. I was hitting my stride. God would have a surprise for me at my membership interview.

In the spring of 1976, when I applied, a question on the form asked about the ability to command another language. Having grown up in the Netherlands I checked the box and wrote, "Dutch, a little bit." Joel

Warkentin was the interviewer. He read through my application, saw that I had a Dutch background, and asked, "Do you still speak some Dutch?" "Yes sir," I explained to him, "I was born in the Netherlands and after our family came across the pond, my mother insisted on speaking Dutch in our new Canadian home. It was her way of connecting us with our heritage and family."

Joel said, "Did you know that we have Bible translation work going on in Suriname?" "No sir," I replied, "where is Suriname?"

"It's on the northern coast of South America, directly north of Brazil. It used to be called Dutch Guiana when it was still a Dutch colony. If you went there, you could easily revive your Dutch. There are two language projects left needing Bible translation. I am the former director of the translation work there and have just returned. I would suggest you write the current director, John Waller, and ask him about a possible assignment to one of those two remaining language groups. Would this interest you?" Joel added.

I floated out of the interview. It was all starting to make sense. What I had experienced as a child and taken as a negative, God was using for good. Being called an ignorant immigrant, or being mocked for my strange accent, or, at the age of six being labeled stupid because I didn't catch a joke in English, was all being turned on its head and into an opportunity to serve the Lord. I thought, "Lord, you really knew what you were doing back there in the Netherlands and later on in Canada. You were taking this scared little boy who was afraid to get on an airplane because he imagined that it would tip over and eject all of its passengers and you are preparing to send him to some strange and foreign place where Dutch is the national language. And you're taking his love for languages to a place where that talent can be used to bring you glory." I didn't see the whole picture yet but things were falling into place. The Netherlands, Dutch, Canada, immigrant, grade school, high school, French, Latin, college, Mexico, Linda, linguistics. What else was needed to complete this picture? What I hadn't figured out yet was how being called a big zero or being told I couldn't learn, fit into the larger picture. God was saving that for later.

A Thousand Times Yes!

As I eagerly returned to my linguistics studies in Dallas, Linda settled back into the routine of teaching her elementary students in Zuni. She quickly discovered that Zuni was the preferred language of communication among the schoolchildren but English was the only allowable vehicle for instruction. Whenever she picked up a word of two of Zuni and used them in the classroom, her students giggled wildly and with admiration for their instructor. These daily happenings confirmed a deep suspicion in her heart; namely, those who are multilingual love to hear their first language. The seed for doing Bible translation in the mother tongue of the world's minority languages was being sown.

We ourselves experienced that love for hearing our own language, years later in 1986, when we traveled via Eurail Pass through Europe. Our ears were constantly bombarded by the plethora of languages used on the continent. French, German, Dutch, Turkish, Chinese, Korean, Russian, and Portuguese were not uncommon. Every once in a while, we heard English being spoken and immediately our eyes and ears sought out the speakers. One time we were on a train near Florence. It was Mark's third birthday and we had bought a small birthday cake to celebrate this important event. He was wearing a pair of red rubber sandals and a blue sailor's outfit. We remember how cute he looked on this special day. He beamed as we started to sing "Happy Birthday". Within seconds, we heard the voices of a middle-aged couple, singing in perfect English, join us. Right there on the express train in Italy, we became instant friends with people from Detroit we didn't even know.

Language has the power to unite and divide, I thought. We shared our small cake and lively conversation followed.

Mark celebrates his 3rd birthday

My correspondence with Linda in New Mexico consisted largely in sending her Wycliffe brochures addressing the need for teachers overseas. Later she confided in me that she was puzzled by the barrage of literature. She thought, "If he's really interested in me, why doesn't he just invite me to the school to see it for myself?" During spring break she made the trek from New Mexico to Dallas and spent several days in my classes. She also was fascinated by the entire linguistic process. The people she met there, the atmosphere at the school, and the growing sense that her love for foreign cultures could easily fit in here, was a wonderful discovery.

She told her friend Lynne, about the weekend's events. Lynne said, "I've been to an SIL training program. I've seen the ratio of guys to girls.

If you want that guy, you had better think about moving to Dallas."
When the time came for Linda to sign her teaching contract for the
following school year, she turned it down and joined me in Texas. I
couldn't have been happier. I was tremendously relieved and elated,
jumping for joy. I was done mailing *Wycliffe Needs Teachers* brochures to
New Mexico.

Linda came from a Dutch background, born in Holland, Michigan.
Her grandfather on her Mom's side was a WWI veteran from a long line
of staunch Calvinists. Grandpa Stegink fought in France but refused to
use his gun to kill the enemy. One day in a heated battle it was his turn
to climb out of the trench to fetch water for his company, a dangerous
proposition making him extremely vulnerable to enemy fire. Reluctantly,
he left his buddies and took his turn at duty, a prayer in his heart. When
he returned, he found his entire company dead in the trench. God's
sovereign care was something he never forgot.

Linda's grandfather on her Dad's side was a descendant of the
Tinholt brothers from the Netherlands, who settled outside of Holland,
Michigan in 1845, to start the village of Graafschap. The brothers
maintained their Dutch Calvinistic traditions and generations later,
Linda was born into that legacy.

God's Word was an important part of her upbringing. Her Dad had
built a special shelf under the dining table for the "Living Bible" that
would be read aloud together after every meal without fail.

In the fall of 1976, Linda came to the Dallas/Fort Worth Metroplex.
Just prior to the start of classes, I asked her Dad for her hand in
marriage. He consented and he gave me the rest of her as well. In a few
weeks, I finally got up the nerve and asked her if she would marry me.
Without any hesitation whatsoever, she threw her arms around me and
said, "Yes, yes, a thousand times yes!" I was overjoyed and could hardly
contain myself. I was ecstatic to finally have a life's partner and we
planned our wedding for August 1977. Money was so scarce that it
would be a while before I could present her with an engagement ring.

We settled into our linguistic classes the fall of 1976. I had concluded
that linguistics and Bible translation would be the perfect combination
and Lin shared that feeling. Her background in education blended easily
into pursuing the literacy aspect so desperately needed in the all-
encompassing project we would shortly embark upon.

Engaged

We were highly motivated about acquiring the necessary education and training in order to launch into our new venture. And neither of us would have to go as a single, a huge relief. When the summer rolled around, we agreed to spend the first few weeks in Dallas to satisfy the non-Indo-European foreign language requirement for my graduate studies. I eagerly jumped into Hebrew but also worked fulltime building homes in the searing heat of Texas. The work atmosphere reminded me of my college days when I did similar work. The off-color jokes hadn't changed and neither had the coarse language. The daily temperatures rose to unbearable levels, and I found myself dehydrating frequently. Going to class for four hours in the morning, then working in the heat for eight hours, and coming home to study Hebrew for another four hours quickly caught up with me. Within weeks we abandoned our plans and decided to head north to the cooler temperatures of Michigan to put the final touches on our wedding plans.

August 13, 1977

BURN YOUR BED

Ed, you can do this!

I cranked the engine but it failed. My faithful Volvo was acting in an unfaithful manner. I cranked it once again. It fired, misfired, and died. "Now what?" I muttered to myself. It was the end of the 1977 spring semester, and Linda and I were anxious to get to Michigan to plan our wedding and then prepare for our last months of training before heading to Suriname. Most of the students had already left for their respective homes, and it was getting lonely on campus. The Texas summer heat was building, and we were stuck in Dallas, with a car that wouldn't cooperate. I tore into the two single-barrel Solex carburetors once again but found nothing unusual. Without the funds to take it to a mechanic, I resorted to my only remaining option: prayer.

I was singing in the shower that evening but it was more from nervousness than praise or thanksgiving. I lifted my arm toward the shower head and prayed, "Lord, what is causing the fuel problem in that car?" Before I could get the words out of my mouth, I was struck by an idea. I recall having looked at the jets that controlled the amount of fuel flowing into the engine, noticing that the orifice they fit into seemed enlarged. Maybe the engine was dying because it was getting *too* much fuel. I let out a loud whoop. "Yes! That's it," I remember saying, as I exited the shower, "That's it!"

The following morning I tackled the car with renewed energy. I dismantled both carburetors, looking carefully at the now-enlarged opening where the jets were located. I borrowed a friend's car, drove to the nearest Volvo dealer in Fort Worth and bought the needed parts. Within an hour I was back, and methodically replaced the parts, while the intense morning sun was burning my back as I worked. With a prayer in my heart, I fired up the engine and she purred like a kitten. God had answered my prayer in the shower. He would be answering many more prayers when it came to cars in the next 20 years. One thing was certain: He was there and He was listening. With joy in our hearts, Linda and I sang all the way to Michigan, again rejoicing in the Lord's goodness.

We spent the rest of the summer up north, splitting our time between Michigan and Ontario. Linda would be in the Great Lake State planning our August wedding and I would be in Ontario working in home construction.

We planned on having an outdoor reception in the flower-laden backyard of the home that Linda grew up in. All week long we kept an eye on the weather, praying for no rain. We were thrilled to have my aunt and uncle come from the Netherlands, new Wycliffe friends from Dallas, Linda's girlfriend Lynne from New Mexico, and all of my siblings and their spouses. My mom was beaming. When Linda walked down the aisle dressed as a southern belle, my heart almost burst. I would get to spend the rest of my life with this godly woman.

The backyard reception came off without a hitch. Linda's mom had been growing flowers in the garden all summer long for the festive occasion and the colorful blooms were everywhere, right down to matching the hues of the bridesmaids' dresses. Her mom had also worked hard preparing different kinds of sweet breads and baked goods. The ladies from the church prepared and served potato salad and other delicacies. My mother showered us with rose petals. My father-in-law's vast vegetable garden drew lots of interest that sunny afternoon. As I looked to the northwest I noticed clouds building up.

I had arranged for a 15-minute flight in a single-engine Cessna to our honeymoon location. Linda's brother had threatened to 'fix' our car prior to the wedding so we parked our vehicle, along with our honeymoon suitcases, at a small airport twenty miles away. As we flew over the outdoor wedding reception at an altitude of 1,000 feet, we could clearly see the remaining guests scurrying here and there, a local squall forcing them indoors. The light band of rain passed quickly, and soon we were on the ground, taxiing right next to our waiting car and drove off to our honeymoon spot. We had successfully foiled my now brother-in-law's threat of spoiling our getaway plans. There would be countless future times when Linda and I would enjoy the sensation of flying in those small aircraft, in ways we could not even begin to imagine.

After the wedding we returned to Texas for my final semester of graduate studies. I planned to finish my course of study in December by taking comprehensive exams and we could make plans to go to Suriname. But it was not to be.

As we settled into our modest, cockroach-infested, one-bedroom apartment in Duncanville, Linda took a job at J.C. Penney's to supplement our limited income and I buckled down to my studies. I had chosen to take comprehensive exams in December to finish my degree rather than write a thesis. It seemed the logical choice since I didn't have a firm topic to pontificate about.

The comps, as they were referred to, would amount to a series of six questions based on the material we had been studying for the past two years. A passing grade was required on five of the six questions to qualify for matriculation. When I took my comps, I had a premonition that I hadn't done as well as I had hoped. And the results bore that out. I had only passed four of the required five questions and it would mean repeating the semester. Shades of yesteryear started to fill my mind, thinking back to the 10th grade. Doubts and feelings of inadequacies became frequent visitors but my adviser had other thoughts. Dr. Bob took me aside and said, "Ed, you can do this. Why don't we meet together every week and we'll go over the material together. I want you to grade some of the papers in the Grammar II class for me. You'll learn a lot about the subject by grading what other students write." I was buoyed by his comments and felt that hope was once again on the horizon.

The spring semester passed by quickly. We had managed to save just enough funds so that Linda could return to her linguistic classes. She loved the literacy courses which would later prove to be most beneficial as we prepared primers and early reading books a few years down the road in Suriname.

Early one morning we walked out of our decrepit apartment to drive to school. Other residents were milling about their cars. The tires on the driver's side of our car had been slashed and multiple cars showed similar damage. A group of teenagers had methodically gone through the parking lot, leaving much damage and frustrated drivers in their wake. The insurance company made good on their promise to supply us with a set of four brand new tires; tires that we surely needed over the next two years as we crisscrossed the country doing our partnership development. The secret hand of the Lord knew how to orchestrate the events of our lives.

The time for comps had arrived again. Dr. Bob reassured me that there wouldn't be a problem this time. He prayed with me, as he had done on a regular basis, and I walked into the testing room with renewed confidence and enthusiasm. The three hours passed quickly and a few weeks later, I was awarded the privilege of a Master of Arts in Linguistics from the University of Texas at Arlington. I thought of my father's 'big zero' comments, and my high school teacher who had suggested I no longer pursue academic training.

A few months later in London, Ontario, I was standing in line at the driver's license bureau when a familiar face and voice approached me. It was Mr. Barrett, my 10th grade music teacher. After exchanging pleasantries he asked me what had happened in the intervening fifteen years. I told him I had recently earned a graduate degree from the University of Texas with the intention of going to Suriname to translate the Scriptures for a people group. He smiled. "Ed," he began, "Do you remember Fred? I met up with him the other day. He played tuba in the school band and was considered to be one of those people least likely to succeed. Fred went to Oxford and just graduated with his Ph.D. in Music Theory. I continue to marvel at all my former students. Well done, Ed. And may God bless you in your endeavors as you head to South America."

Ja'mal Haven

"You will be spending four months in Mexico's Jungle Camp. There you'll learn to live in an environment where most of your daily routine will be stripped away and replaced with unique opportunities to trust God. All new Wycliffe members go through this training to prepare them for living in places where Bible translation predominantly takes place," the instructor told us. Combining the words 'jungle' and 'camp' sounded both exciting and daunting. I had experienced this same Jungle Camp setting some four years earlier but only for a short week. Four months seemed like an incredibly long time, but the adventure appealed to us. Would we be ready for this last stage before going to Suriname to do Bible translation? We would soon know.

In the fall of 1978 we were deposited, along with several dozen other campers and their children back in southern Chiapas, a stone's throw from the Guatemalan border. The 20-minute airplane ride from San Cristobal de Las Casas to Yaxoquintela seemed less harrowing this time around but thrilling nevertheless. I had accepted that mission aviation was not what God had intended for me, however, that didn't lessen the thrill of flying. Every time I strapped myself into one of those little aircraft, my heart would leap into my throat in sheer excitement.

This session of Jungle Camp, including staff, totaled 90 people, a large group considering the logistics and coordination needed to successfully run a camp of this size and diversity. This was not a day camp or a week long summer camp or a ten-day jaunt into the Amazon rainforest. This camping style was meant to prepare us for the rigors of living overseas in often impoverished or extreme conditions. Today's reality shows don't begin to compare with the experiences of Mexico's Jungle Camp. This was no game.

As we settled into our routine, it became obvious that we were both meant for this. The four-month experience was divided into three phases: Main Base, Advanced Base, and Village Living. Main Base and Village Living lasted six weeks each and Advanced Base would last for a week. We reasoned that if we could survive Jungle Camp, we could probably survive living anywhere. Our skills and faith would be tested, though.

The engine's roar was unmistakable as it cascaded off the valley's walls but why would an airplane be flying over Jungle Camp on Christmas Day 1978? Was there an emergency? We rushed out of the dining hall to see not one but both of MAF's Cessna 185s making low circling passes over Yax. Something was ejected from the lead plane. A small parachute opened up and slowly drifted to earth. Within seconds we recognized it as a large Santa doll floating down to the waiting campers. A cheer went up. When the planes landed on the grass strip, the pilots and their families extracted themselves from the aircraft and we helped carry the remaining cargo. Cases of ice cold Cokes were unloaded from the belly pods. To enjoy an ice cold soft drink, here in the middle of the southern Mexican jungle, on Christmas Day no less, was an experience none of us would ever forget.

Jungle Camp came with its own built-in character builders. The slaughtering of cows and chickens being one example. Whenever a cow was butchered, which happened about every 10-14 days, to feed everyone in the camp, it meant two things: a lot of work for many people and, liver and onions. Many campers turned up their noses at the thought of eating liver but Linda and I had grown up enjoying this delicacy. Heart and tongue likewise, were normally eschewed by most but some of us feasted on it.

Learning to live without electricity, flush toilets, running water, and other modern conveniences we take for granted was a challenge. For example, in order to prevent sickness, all drinking water had to be boiled for at least 15 minutes and then naturally cooled. This task would become one of the most important chores that campers were assigned.

Everywhere we went we walked. The pounds rolled off with ease. New living skills were acquired daily. We learned how to give injections, string up army hammocks, cook and bake over a wood fire using cast iron skillets and Dutch ovens, paddle and maneuver large 1,000 pound dugout canoes, and swim in swiftly flowing rivers. At the same time we would be trying to learn Spanish and Tzeltal, two languages that were vastly different from one another. Spanish was the national language of Mexico but Jungle Camp was in the state of Chiapas where many different indigenous languages were spoken, languages that were native to these valleys long before Spanish conquistadors ever set foot in Central America.

After Main Base was accomplished, we would spend a week at Advanced Base, putting into practice all of our newly acquired skills before heading off to the Village Living phase. The word spread quickly that Survival Training would be part of the Village Living phase. This would mean several days in the jungle by oneself, setting up a shelter and learning to live off the land. Exciting times were ahead.

The Village Living experience would become Jungle Camp's four-month capstone. We were divided into family units and lived with local Tzeltal families in their huts. In some cases, small structures would have to be built to accommodate us campers. The staff asked us which village we would like to live in. We told them that Victoria sounded like the perfect place. This village was the furthest away from Main Base and would present us with the maximum challenge. When it came time to announce our village allocations, Victoria was not on the list. A logistical problem meant the village was unable to accommodate us. Instead, we would be assigned to live in La Union, a tiny village that was the closest of all to Jungle Camp, directly across the river. We were shocked. How would we learn anything being so close to Main Base, so close that we could hear the dinner bell ringing to bring the next group of campers to the dining hall? God was at work demonstrating His powerful love for us in ways that we hadn't expected.

"Radio Mundo!" The announcer's voice crackled through the tinny speaker of the battery-powered transistor radio. The 'r's rolled off his tongue like marbles clattering on a granite floor. I always had trouble rolling my 'r's but for Linda, making those tongue tips sounds, those alveolar 'r's, was natural. In the future I would teach her how to make uvular 'r's, the way northern Europeans did.

The announcement from the radio meant it must be 4 A.M. Village living had begun in earnest. The listener cranked up the volume as La

Union sprang to life. A few feet from our heads we could hear the 'pat, pat, pat' of tortillas being made, as expert hands worked at shaping the corn-based delicacies. The aroma drove us out of our warm sleeping bags and within minutes we sat silently on logs enjoying strong hot coffee served in white enamel mugs accompanied by the fresh tortillas. In the hurry to find a village for us, Jungle Camp staff had arranged for us to live in La Union, across a swiftly flowing river from Main Base and up a steep embankment. There was no suitable hut for us to live in so an abandoned corn crib was quickly converted into our living space. The structure had a mud stove, dirt floor, walls made of sticks and branches and a thatch roof, giving shelter to mice, rats, and other creatures, too numerous to mention. But it was home. The Tzeltal word for jungle is "Ja'mal" (ha'-mall). I made a small wooden sign that read "Ja'mal Haven" and hung it over the narrow doorway. As small and crowded as our little dwelling was, we were determined to make the most of our time in this tiny enclave. Many adventures lay ahead.

From time to time we would walk to nearby villages to visit other campers or to improve our Tzeltal language learning skills. Frequently, rivers or streams would have to be crossed during our treks. At most crossing points, one could usually find a dugout canoe. They were hewn from a single tree, measuring up to twenty feet or more in length and three feet across. Maneuvering one of these 1,000 pound beasts could be a challenge. The only way to pilot a dugout is by standing up. Jungle Camp staff had provided excellent instruction in their handling, and we quickly learned to make 'J' and 'C' strokes with the heavy wooden paddles to direct the otherwise unwieldy craft. Frequently, there would be no canoe available or it would be tied up to a tree on the other side of the stream, forcing me to strip down, swim across the river to fetch it, in order to bring Linda across. It was unthinkable, in Tzeltal culture, for a man to get his pants wet, and I would soon learn this lesson in a most embarrassing manner.

Navigating a 1000 lb. dugout canoe

Water from the nearby river had to be carried in buckets. In La Union, one could go down to the river's edge and haul water back up the steep embankment, or to a smaller stream, closer to the village but up an impossibly steep hill. Carrying water was considered women's work, and I never saw a local man participating in it. The village women would climb down the hill with their buckets and their laundry and stand, knee-deep in the river, washing their clothes on the rocks while chatting. When they were done, they would fill a bucket with river water, place it on top of their heads, grab their newly laundered clothes and trudge up the embankment. It was heavy and hard work. I reasoned that a man could carry water just as well as a woman, maybe not on top of his head, but at least he could carry two buckets back to the hut to use for cooking, etc. We had already been taught how to purify the river water. It meant boiling it and then letting it cool for about 24 hours. Simply opening a faucet and getting potable water seemed like a miracle. Living took a lot of time, as we discovered daily.

One morning before breakfast I grabbed two buckets and decided to surprise Linda by getting water from the nearby stream. I angled my way past the rocky outcropping and within minutes I was at the water's edge, dipping my buckets into the cool, swiftly flowing water. "This is easy," I thought, "why hadn't I come here before? Why didn't the villagers come here?" My pants were perfectly dry at this point but as I hoisted the buckets out of the water, I accidentally dislodged something beneath the surface. A small hollow gourd, the size of a softball, popped up and started to float downstream. I quickly abandoned my buckets and plunged into the cold water to retrieve the empty gourd. In so doing, I disturbed other gourds, some as large as soccer balls. They, too, popped out of the water. They had been placed there by the villagers, jammed against the rocks to keep them submerged to season them. I was running wildly now, downstream, trying desperately to retrieve every last gourd that had surfaced, making their way to a small waterfall. I lunged after the last one and struggled to the shore, with the last of the precious gourds in my possession. My pants were wet all the way up to my waist. How was I going to explain this to the villagers?

I plodded back to where the gourds had originally been placed, doing my best to make the site look undisturbed. I waded into the cool water, my pants sloshing around my ankles. I refilled the buckets, and struggled up the steep embankment to the center of the village. The hill was steeper than I had imagined and the water continued to slosh out of the metal containers. When I arrived at the top of the hill, all eyes were on me. I slowly made my way around the sizable group of men, who were doing their best to control their laughter, but it was no use. Here was the dumb gringo, doing woman's work, carrying buckets, not on his head, but in his hands. The buckets were barely half full, and his pants were completely and totally sodden with river water. A loud roar of laughter erupted from the men and women alike. I had one thought and only one thought: why not throw the water right into their faces and get it over with? Instead, I set the half empty buckets down and joined them in their fun. I learned to laugh at myself that day. There would be more days ahead when I would feel like a neophyte in this fascinating culture.

As the weeks of Village Living unfolded, we couldn't wait for the day when we would arrive in South America and commence the work of Bible translation for the Javanese of Suriname. Our Jungle Camp experience would be over by the 1st of April. We gave ourselves four additional months preparation to raise the necessary prayer and financial partners. August 1 sounded like a good date and we settled on it. In the meantime, we had a few 'minor' items on our Jungle Camp adventure checklist that remained undone. Of these, Survival Training loomed the largest. When would the staff come to get us to experience what it would be like to be stranded or lost in the jungle for several days? Since the first day of Jungle Camp, every camper knew this would be the real test, and it was the most frequent topic of conversation among past, present, and future campers. When staff finally hiked up the hill to our village, we knew what the announcement would be. Would we be prepared? We would soon find out.

Mail pickup and delivery to our villages was once a week. Any news from the home front was especially welcome. It was disconcerting to see staff return with the previous week's mail that bore insufficient postage. There was no easy method of weighing a letter in the jungle. There was a small postal scale back at main base but Village Living campers were discouraged from visiting Main Base, except in emergencies. I made a miniature balance scale using pieces of rough sawn wood, and small nuts and bolts as counterweights. We were thrilled to conquer this challenge. Jungle Camp was helping us in more ways than we could imagine. To this day, I keep a small, electronic postage scale in the office.

Wayne Huff was exhausted by the time he had climbed up to our Ja'mal Haven but we were thrilled to see him. He had come for a short visit to encourage and listen to us. Was there anything we needed? Were we comfortable? Were we able to handle the stress of living in this rather impoverished situation? The questions just kept on coming and we relished his time with us. Wayne was part of Jungle Camp staff and made the rounds to every camper. His half hour visit was far too short as we poured out our hearts to this humble servant. He ended his visit by praying over us, for God's perfect will and protection and future plans. His visit stands out as a highlight of Jungle Camp.

The word quickly spread that Survival Hike would be conducted on the second-to-the-last week of Village Living. Soon, a visitor from Main Base dragged himself up the steep hill to our little cabana to announce the long awaited and dreaded event. I strapped on my machete and other necessary items, kissed Linda good-bye and followed the visitor back down the hill to the growing group of nervous men. Survival Hike would be the ultimate test for us jungle campers, and we would be banking on all of our newly acquired skills to accomplish this feat. I had not forgotten to tuck my pocket Bible into my backpack. It would become my constant companion during the four-day ordeal. When we arrived at the general location, we separated and started to set up our camps. We were far enough away from fellow campers to not see each other but close enough to hear each other chopping wood.

The first order of business was to build a shelter large enough to house a stick bed for four nights. The second was to build and maintain a proper campfire. Dry firewood would not be easy to find in this damp setting but it was essential to have a fire going all the time to prepare whatever food could be found and, more importantly, to stay warm at night. If the campfire was positioned correctly, you could use a large polyethylene sheet as a reflector and bounce the warm rays from your fire back into the sleeping area. It would take some doing to get it all set up before nightfall. The first night I struggled with the fire. It was close enough to my bed but the wind was wrong and I was awake most of the night because of smoke in the little shelter. I would have to re-position my tent in the morning to take advantage of the prevailing wind.

The following morning I was up early, ate the last of the granola Linda had managed to stuff into my backpack and went on the hunt for food. I found a small stream with some snails and dug them out of their shells. Then I cooked them over my open fire. Although not particularly tasty, they were a good source of protein.

Next, I went about the task of rearranging my sleeping area. I switched it around 180 degrees and repositioned my fire. By noon, the job was complete. The large polyethylene sheet was draped over some poles, angled back against the bed and then stretched over the sleeping area. My bed was about a foot off the ground and the fire less than three feet from it. I would be able to add wood to the star-shaped fire without having to crawl out of my warm sleeping bag in the middle of the night. I secured the tarp with vines I had cut from neighboring trees. That night and the remaining nights, I slept like a baby in my renovated arrangement. I was so proud of myself; all of the training had paid off handsomely. In the future I would remember that staying warm and staying calm were the most essential elements to survival.

For the sake of the experiment, staff told us to consider the local people hostile. We were not to interact or communicate with them. For the first two days, I went along with the rules. But on the third day while gathering firewood, I encountered two Tzeltal men fishing in a nearby stream. I watched them from a distance as they pulled small fish out of the water. By now my empty stomach was growling as the snails and other food I could scrounge up just weren't cutting it.

Every now and then they paused to drink from a plastic jug which I reasoned was their lunch. Since this was survival, I rationalized that finding food was most essential. I approached the men and gestured towards their container, offering them a few fishing hooks as payment. They gladly accepted the hooks and I drank deeply from the jug. It contained mats, a corn-based gruel. It was nourishing but had a powerful, pungent odor and I wondered if I would get sick. I made my way back to my little campground and continued gathering firewood and snails and other edible plants. By the afternoon, I had developed a good case of diarrhea. Thankfully it was short lived but I had paid the price for not following Jungle Camp rules.

As I lay in my bed that evening, I concluded that the hardest part of being on survival hike was not the lack of food, not the lack of comfort, and not the lack of having enough to do. No, it was the lack of people contact that was the most difficult part for me. Having a Bible was wonderful and provided many hours of companionship but having not one other person to talk to took a toll on me. Nowhere did that manifest itself more than on survival hike.

That night I slept like a log but in the morning I awoke to strange noises. Men's voices could be heard coming through the jungle. But they were not speaking Tzeltal. They were the voices of the other campers on survival hike. As they approached my little campground, I noticed they were escorting David, a fellow camper. His head was swollen to about twice normal size, and he was in need of immediate medical help. Evidently Dave had made his bed out of *cheching* twigs and also used them in his campfire. This wood, when handled or burned, released a chemical that could cause a severe reaction if you were allergic to it, and Dave had fallen victim to it. Jungle Camp staff ended survival hike for the men prematurely. I quickly dismantled my little campground. I had grown to enjoy my surroundings, proud of my little setup but was more than ready to return to Linda.

We spent several days talking about the shared experiences of our survival hikes. The women had banded together while the men had been required to stay apart. Linda said they found several snakes, managed to kill them and roasted the meat over the open fire. Boiling snails in a canteen was not appealing and eating leaves proved caustic. She found little sleep because her campfire's smoke drifted into the shelter. Nothing, however, compared with the chocolate bars that appeared out of nowhere at the end. We knew that if we found ourselves in a similar situation someday, we would be better prepared to handle it. It had turned into a faith-and-confidence-building exercise.

With just a couple of weeks to go in Jungle Camp, we prepared ourselves for heading to Suriname to start our long awaited task of Bible translation. We took out our calendar and circled August 1.

Jungle Camp was over but the lessons learned and the friendships made would last us a lifetime. Suriname loomed large on our radar screen now. Would we finally get to do what we had waited for so long? In four months we would find out.

The Coup That Couldn't Happen

Those four months passed by all too quickly. We said good-bye to family and friends and boarded an aging DC-8 in Miami for Suriname. We hopscotched through the Caribbean, landing briefly at exotic destinations including Curacao, Trinidad, and Guyana before setting foot on Suriname's soil for the first time. The oppressive heat and unrelenting humidity overwhelmed us. It was midnight, August 1, 1979.

We didn't consider at the time how sacrificial this may have been for Linda's parents. The day before, we had gathered around the family picnic table her Dad had made. We were sitting in the shade of the large beech trees, eating a delicious home-cooked meal made by her Mom. We all knew it would be the last meal together for a while but nothing was said. Perhaps that thought was too painful. At midnight severe thunderstorms rolled in off Lake Michigan, keeping us awake most of the night. The blinding lightning flashes lit up the spare bedroom we were staying in. Storm after storm rumbled through the area. The lightning and thunder continued through the night as we anticipated our morning departure.

Now several weeks later in Paramaribo, Suriname's capital, John Waller, the director of the SIL work, made a remark that caught us off guard. He said, "Welcome to Suriname. Most of the Javanese people live along the coast, spread over some 40 villages. Find a village to live in to learn their language and culture."

Eventually we found that one-in-forty village and our small Dessa home, via our friends Marius and Kati, nephew of the lurah headman.

We signed the rental agreement for our village home and within two weeks, rumors started flying around Suriname that a coup was in the making. The Army had been on strike for a number of weeks, threatening a takeover, but the vast majority of Surinamers denied it could happen in their beloved country. It was February 25, 1980, when Buck and I left Paramaribo for the 35-minute drive to Dessa, the Javanese village where Linda and I settled down to learn the culture and language of this displaced Asian people group. Buck, a man from Guyana, the country directly to the west, had left his family behind and come in search of work, hoping for a better life. He agreed to help me build a small footbridge over the narrow ditch leading to our village abode.

We left at 6:00 A.M., getting an early start to avoid the hottest part of the day. Traffic was strangely sparse as we wove our way to the village. It seemed eerily quiet that February morning. The sweat poured down our faces as we unloaded the railroad ties that would constitute the foundation of our bridge. We worked hard throughout most of the morning, taking frequent water breaks to alleviate our thirst. The ten-foot ties barely spanned the ditch but they were sufficient. Now we would be able to park our canary-yellow Honda next to the unpainted house.

Village people shuffled by, some stopping to watch the action. Every now and then we heard them speak a word or two. Their words were indistinct but one word stood out, "War!" Repeatedly people came by and uttered that one word. Some added the phrase, "in the city." Buck and I largely ignored them, racing against the noonday sun to complete our bridge building project. When we looked to the north we saw billows of smoke rising from the capital city. We figured something was brewing but we were largely clueless. A major event was unfolding that threatened to drastically alter our plans to do Bible translation in this tropical country. We had arrived six months earlier, assured by the local populace that Suriname was a peace-loving, largely pacifistic country. Tolerance was shown among the many people groups from all over the world that had made their home here.

Several African people groups comprised the slave population that were forced to work on the many plantations that dotted the landscape in the 1600s. Another people group from India, the Hindustanis, came as indentured servants to work those same plantations after emancipation was declared in 1863. But to satisfy the growing need for additional laborers, some 30,000 contract workers from Indonesia were also brought over, starting in 1889 and ending in 1939, at the onset of World War II. This last and final group would become our reason for leaving our families in North America and initiate Bible translation in the steamy jungle.

Buck and I struggled with the heavy creosote-saturated railroad ties. When we were satisfied with the job, we drove the borrowed Chevy Blazer over the newly built bridge to test the quality of our workmanship. It held! Delighted with our efforts, we packed up our few tools and headed back to the city where Linda would be waiting with supper. As we drove onto the main road that led from the international airport back to Paramaribo, we were confronted by a strange sight. The roads were practically devoid of traffic but military vehicles were everywhere. Still puzzled, we turned on the radio, surprised to hear military music. Tuning to other radios stations produced the same result. What was happening? My mind started spinning. Surely there hadn't been a coup, or had there? Every now and then we were forced through a military checkpoint that hadn't been there in the morning. Was it possible that this peaceful country had been overtaken? Many Surinamers had reassured me that a coup just couldn't happen here. The military had threatened to go on strike for better wages and working conditions but there was hardly anyone in the country that believed they would carry out their threats. Perhaps it had, in fact, taken place.

We were met with more roadblocks and military checkpoints, more frequent the closer we got to the city. Buck was clearly anxious. He, like so many thousands upon thousands of other Guyanese, had come to Suriname in search of employment, crossing the border without possessing the proper paperwork. They found day jobs and worked hard to establish themselves. The government largely ignored them because they filled an important sector in the labor force. But the anxiety of deportation was showing on Buck's face.

I had my own anxieties. There was a .22 caliber handgun in the glove compartment belonging to the owner of the borrowed truck, and we were certain that a vehicle search would uncover the weapon. I prayed silently that we would not be stopped. As we navigated our way through the back streets to avoid further checkpoints, both Buck and I heaved a huge sigh of relief upon reaching our destination. Linda was enormously relieved to see me as I was to see her.

"There's been a military coup!" she blurted out, "Did you hear the news as you drove in?" "Well," I stammered, "I knew there was trouble but we couldn't make out what had taken place. We hadn't listened to the radio all day, except when we drove back from the village. People kept coming by the village house all day talking about war and events going on in the city but we never connected the dots. What's the latest?" "Sixteen non-commissioned officers overtook the government this morning, shortly after you left for the village. Our colleagues have been praying for you and Buck all day long, praying that you would be able to make it back into the city. I have never been so worried in all of my life. The military has declared a dawn-to-dusk curfew. I'm so glad you made it back home in time. Were you stopped at all?"

Over the next few weeks, as the military junta made their desires known, our SIL branch leadership huddled together frequently, trying to devise a plan that would ensure the ongoing activity of Bible translation in the country. But there were further regulations put into place by the military regime that gave the appearance that foreigners, such as ourselves, might be targeted. Splinter groups, frequently consisting of disgruntled soldiers, armed themselves and attempted to stage counter coups, all of them unsuccessful. Nevertheless, it made life miserable for everyone. In one counter coup attempt, major electrical transmission lines were cut and electricity had to be rationed.

We found ourselves with an uncertain work schedule. We needed electricity for our offices and our homes. The SIL branch invested in a large generator that could be used to keep us going during electrical outages. All kinds of new military regulations were put into effect. One of the new rules meant that no one was allowed to own foreign currency of any kind. This would have a severe impact on the entire business of Bible translation since the majority of the funds came from outside the country. As the regulations became more stringent, the branch made contingency plans to move the entire Bible translation operation to another location. Several options were put on the table.

A couple of years later, in December 1982, 15 outstanding citizens who had expressed their dissatisfaction with the military regime, were summarily rounded up and executed. The victims included labor union leaders, radio announcers, lawyers, journalists, sports writers, and other well-known Surinamers. The general population became mutes as people feared for their lives if they protested. Many daily items were rationed, and we at SIL started to import 20 and 40 foot containers of food and supplies from Miami. The situation appeared to get worse but we were functioning, keeping a low profile.

Until 1975 when it finally gained its independence, Suriname was a Dutch colony. Before that time, Surinamers carried Dutch passports and moved easily between Suriname and the Netherlands without restrictions. Many Surinamers of every ethnic stripe, including the Javanese, had found their way to the Netherlands and established communities there. The SIL branch leadership reasoned that moving the operation to the Netherlands would be a viable option, and because of my Dutch-speaking background, asked me to investigate the possibility of the branch doing Bible translation from there.

As I started my research I happened upon an article written by C.S. Lewis. The article was titled *Learning in War-Time* written in 1939 as World War II was about to explode on the world scene. Following are two excerpts quoted from that lecture.

Plausible reasons have never been lacking for putting off all merely cultural activities until some imminent danger has been averted or some crying injustice put right. But humanity long ago chose to neglect those plausible reasons. They wanted knowledge and beauty now, and would not wait for the suitable moment that never came.

There are always plenty of rivals to our work. We are always falling in love or quarreling, looking for jobs or fearing to lose them, getting ill and recovering, following public affairs. If we let ourselves, we shall always be waiting for some distraction or other to end before we can really get down to our work. The only people who achieve much are those who want knowledge so badly that they seek it while the conditions are still unfavorable. Favorable conditions never come.

As I read and prayed, a thread appeared that has since become a guiding principle for much of my life. We can't wait for all the conditions to be right before forging ahead on a project. If we wait for all of our ducks to line up, we may be waiting in vain. If we wait for all the planets to line up before making a move, we may never start. Collectively, the decision was made that it would be best to remain in country to continue with the work of Bible translation in the seven language projects we had so heavily invested in. Yes, there would be trials and troubles but the

Lord never promised us an easy road; rather, he said that trial and tribulation could be expected when we pledged to follow Him.

With new purpose and determination, we viewed the current situation as an opportunity to trust God for all of our needs. It welded us together as a unit and we started looking after each other as never before. We invited our language helpers to participate in our food convoys, supplying them and their families with some of the necessities of life. Through the rumblings of uncertainty, food shortages, power outages, counter coups and continual bad news, the Suriname branch persevered. When the heavy bans were finally lifted, we all breathed a collective sigh of relief and completed the jobs that we had come to do. Of the 20 years Linda and I spent in Suriname, 17 of them were under some sort of military rule. Democracy, more or less, returned in the late 1990s.

Already in Trouble

Getting a start at living in our small village of Dessa, after building the bridge with Buck, had challenges of its own. Working outside in the stifling heat trying to make the house livable, took a toll on both of us. Linda often felt depleted of all her energy, and would have to rest on the 2 x 10s stretched across a pair of old sawhorses. One of our colleagues suggested, "Are you pregnant?" When she went to the clinic, the doctor confirmed it. We were so surprised but delighted at the same time. We'd be starting out village life with a newborn.

Linda's parents came for a visit just prior to David's birth to help set up our village home and learn about our new surroundings. Mom helped Linda sew some maternity clothes and Dad worked with me in the hot sun mixing cement for a set of steps to the indoor kitchen. When the delivery day finally arrived, Linda's friend Lynne came from the States to stay with us for a couple of weeks. My own Mom followed shortly thereafter, eager to hold her third grandchild and fulfill her dream of visiting the mission field. She walked David in her arms up and down the sandy car path in front of our home singing her Dutch Psalms, making friends along the way. It was a delight that these beautiful brown-skinned people knew some Dutch and therefore she could use her mother tongue to begin to relate. The young girls started referring to her as 'lieve Oma', loving Grandma. After Mom left to go back home to Canada we were once again on our own, neophytes, to care for a baby. We relied heavily on Dr. Spock's baby book. But having an infant opened up many doors for relating with the people. Raising a baby couldn't be that much different between cultures, could it?

Dr. Spock said babies sometimes cry because they're just tired and it's good for them to develop their lungs. So we didn't worry too much about David's cries at night in his little crib just around the corner from our bedroom door, five feet from our bed. We would be questioned the next morning, however, by neighbors who said, "I heard your baby cry." And surprise was expressed that we let the poor baby sleep 'alone' instead of in our bed. Word also spread quickly that the white American *nursed* her baby and didn't give a bottle with formula or sweet tea.

One time our little infant got sick with a temperature that spiked up to 104 degrees. We were nervous young parents driving out into the night to find an open clinic for some antibiotics. A shot was given and things settled down quickly but it was a night to be remembered going out past the curfew hour while still under military regime. We thought of our neighbors who would travel by bromfiets (moped) with three,

David opened up the doors to many village homes

sometimes four members of the family on the bike at once, often having to wait for the tropical rain to stop before pressing on.

Another time David contracted a cold with a stuffy nose that made breathing uncomfortable and fussiness. We decided to ask the Javanese nurse at the end of the car path what could be done. First she asked if the baby was a boy or girl. "A boy," I told her. "Well then," she said, "the mother is the one that needs to put her mouth over the baby's nose to suction out the mucus." I came home and said to Linda, "It's your job."

Peep, peep, peep, peep, peep! The incessant noise was deafening as we stood outside the wire-enclosed barn, fascinated by the thousands of chicklets inside the enclosure. But our fascination quickly turned sour as we heard an angry voice behind us, yelling an expletive-laden warning, "What do you think you're doing? This is no place for snooping around. If you don't leave this instant, I'm going to call the police! Do you hear me?"

Linda and I had lived in Dessa for just a few of weeks, trying to learn the unwritten Suriname Javanese language. It was our habit to walk around the village practicing the few words we did know in order to gain fluency. But these angry words were not Javanese words; they were in Dutch, my first language. When I turned to look who was screaming at us, I encountered a man of short stature. He was not Javanese. As he continued his verbal assault, I turned to Linda and whispered to her, "You had better head for home. I'll see if I can quiet this guy down." But the man was not to be consoled and continued his barrage. "Who do you think you are walking onto my property without permission? I'm trying to make a living here, and you're not going to disrupt my business. Now get off my property as fast as you can!" The veins in his neck stood out as he shouted. "I apologize, sir. We're leaving as fast as we can," I offered.

As we walked the short distance to our two-room home, beads of sweat formed on my face. The midday sun was beating down. That, along with the constant high humidity, normally confined our village walks to the early evening. "Lin," I started, "I can't believe what just happened. Here we are, just a few weeks in the village and we're already in trouble. We really need the Lord's help on this one. An incident like this could easily ruin our opportunity to learn this language and jeopardize our living in the village. Lord, please help us." A verse came to mind. "A quietly given gift soothes an irritable person; a heartfelt present cools a hot temper." (Proverbs 21:14, The Message). I shared the verse with Linda and asked her, "What could we possibly give him to calm him down?"

"I'll bake him some cinnamon rolls," she said. That sounded like a good idea but I was worried that I had made a blunder that would make the gossip rounds in the small village and that I had just blown our chance to leave a favorable impression for the sake of the Gospel. Linda worked hard the next day making the cinnamon rolls. The aroma wafted out of our little home. We often wondered what our next door neighbors thought of the strange food we prepared, but our palates were also quickly learning favorites among their strange food.

Once when I commented to a neighbor about the wonderful and flavorful cassava chips made in the village, we were startled by a loud knock on our front door. When we opened it, the greeter was gone but a large trash bag had been set by the front door. How rude, I thought, to leave trash on my doorstep. But when we opened it, we discovered an entire bag full of freshly fried cassava chips, seasoned with garlic. We were beginning to like our neighbors.

The cinnamon rolls were now ready and early the next morning with them in hand, I walked back to the chicken man's house. How was I going to be received? I was surely taking a chance that it may not work out well but I had faith in the Scripture that the gift would not be rejected. As I walked onto his property, the front door opened and he ran out, yelling at me to leave immediately, and threatening once again to call the police. I had been hiding the plateful of rolls behind my back and when I presented them to him, he said, in shock, "What's that?"

I said, "I've come to apologize for what happened yesterday. Please accept these as a gift. We promise never to set foot on your property again." He lifted the tinfoil, exposing the rolls and the aroma caught his nostrils. In an instant, his entire demeanor changed. He gulped and said, "Please come in. I want you to meet my wife and kids. I married a lovely Javanese woman some years ago, and I'm trying to make a living here in the village raising chickens. Where are you from? What are you doing here in the Dessa? And how come you speak Dutch so well? Please, please, come in and meet my family."

The Javanese are friendly and hospitable people. Whenever we were walking down the sandy car path for a stroll or a trip to the corner store we would hear 'Mampir, mampir', please stop and visit. A child would be sent to the store for a liter of Cola in a glass bottle and then to a

Linda collecting language data to decipher the sound system

neighbor with a refrigerator to buy a block of ice. The host would break the ice in her hand with the dull side of a large knife and the broken pieces would clunk into a glass to make the cold Coca-Cola even colder in this tropical heat. We'd sit on their cooler cement porch floor catching a little breeze and learn a few more words or phrases. Our baby was a center of attraction and made an easy way to relate when words were few. Mothers wanted to wrap him in their cotton batik 'slindang' and jiggle him up and down until Linda thought he must be craving a little peace and quiet. Since their phonetics were different than ours, they pronounced his name as 'Japit' rather than David. We were starting to feel welcome and more comfortable in our new village setting.

BURN YOUR BED

East or West?

"Layat, layat, layat." Linda and I rushed to the front door of our little village house and watched as the man rode by on his old worn out cruiser bike, intoning words we didn't understand. He made his rounds throughout the entire village, circled back and repeated the routine. We wondered what it meant. Within a few hours we noticed women walking down the dusty, sandy road past our house carrying bowls in slings around their shoulders. Probably food, we reasoned. We watched in fascination but had no idea that an oft-repeated important village event was unfolding in front of our eyes. It would be a while before we would understand.

A few weeks later it happened again. "Layat, layat, layat, Paiman Pawiro. Layat, Paiman Pawiro." The bicyclist pedaled hard on the sandy track, announcing the death of our neighbor. Paiman had been one of our several language helpers. At 36, he was far too young to depart from this world, leaving behind his wife and three sons.

We made our way to the house just a few doors down and found a quiet and somber mood inside. People were sitting on the floor around the perimeter of the living room. In one corner a couple of bed sheets hung from the ceiling, concealing the dead man's body from view. Soft chatter, mixed with the clanging of pots and pans, emanated from the outdoor kitchen in back. Within minutes, three Islamic priests emerged, walked over to the corner of the room, and parted the sheets exposing my friend's lifeless body. The sheets were pulled down and used to wrap Paiman's body. Gently it was carried outside and laid down on a makeshift table. The noonday sun was directly overhead, beating down mercilessly on the trio of priests. They loosened the sheets and began washing the corpse in blue-dyed water. A few indistinct words were spoken by the priests, none of which I could understand but it sounded like Arabic. Many village rituals were performed in Arabic; few villagers understood the words but even fewer would admit it. Memorized phrases had been handed down from one generation to the next. The priests used the proper intonation, and the listeners knew exactly how and when to respond. These were well-oiled and practiced routines. A later discovery didn't surprise me at all: the priests were largely illiterate.

The body was once again wrapped up in the sheets and placed in an old coffin. The lid was placed loosely on top and the complete assembly was hoisted onto the shoulders of four men who trudged under their heavy load to the nearby cemetery. Two men, both wielding machetes, preceded the small troupe, swinging their tools to scare off any evil spirits that might consider following us. I'm sure they felt threatened. No women were allowed beyond this point. As we silently approached the graveyard, I could see the hole that had been dug earlier that morning. It was barely four feet deep. The coffin was placed on the ground, the lid removed, the wrapped-up body taken out and gently lowered into the grave. It would be foolish to bury good wood into the ground. That coffin would be used and reused many times in the future.

No sooner had the frame found the bottom of the shallow pit when a priest jumped in and grabbed the deceased's head. I glanced around and noticed that all the graves had been dug in a north-south orientation. The head was placed at the north end of the grave. The priest commenced to shout into the dead man's ear, "There is no god but Allah and Mohammed is his prophet. There is no god but Allah and Mohammed is his prophet." Over and over again, the priest shouted the Arabic phrase into Paiman's deaf ears. I turned to my neighbor, and said, "It's too late." He looked at me in disbelief and said, "Silitmu mambu." I was still pretty new in the language. Anything I didn't understand I wrote down in my ever present notepad and I promised myself I would find out what it meant.

As the priest continued to shout the age-old phrase, the men standing around the miserable opening started to talk and tell jokes. Sex jokes were not uncommon. When the priest finished, he grabbed Paiman's head, turned to the circle of men and asked, "East or west?" A small discussion ensued. Eventually someone said, "East." The priest turned the head into an easterly direction, covered it with the sheet and extracted himself from the grave. We grabbed shovels and heaped the freshly dug dirt onto the body. As the dirt mounded up, flower petals were strewn over top. Someone took an old black umbrella, opened it up and shoved it into the heaping pile of dirt, warding off any evil spirits that might be lurking in the vicinity. The entire ritual lasted no more than twenty minutes. Except for the joking session, not a single word of Javanese had been uttered, only Arabic. Did anyone at all understand even one thing that had just taken place? I attended many funerals in the four years we lived in the village but after my first one, I already knew that the Javanese desperately needed to have God's Word in their own language. To be buried without hope, was not an option. I redoubled my efforts to learn the language.

Our first attempt in training Bible translation principles

Attending more funerals deepened my resolve. They were depressing, to say the least, but they were rich for language learning. In the absence of women, facts of village life that were not normally discussed anywhere else, emerged effortlessly. But the east/west issue continued to elude me. Why did the priest insist on asking whether the man was east or west? Why was this distinction so important to them? There had to be a reason but I was utterly stymied.

When a new home was constructed in the village, the owner first went to the mosque and asked the priests when the construction could start. Immediate payment was expected. There could be severe consequences if one initiated construction on the wrong date. Evil would certainly befall any individual attempting such a foolish move. There were spirits to placate, gods to appease, and traditions to be upheld. The overriding factor, however, was that the priests had to somehow make a living.

The longer we lived in the village, the more things became evident to us. Some newly constructed homes stood empty for three years. Only the priest could determine the date of occupancy. Visits to the mosque were frequent, seeking permission for occupancy. It occurred to me that all of the homes had their main entrance on the north or south side of the dwelling. East? West? No, it must be something else. I quietly roamed the village, asking about the east/west situation but no answers were forthcoming. I surmised it had something to do with their worldview since it was the last act of one's life before being committed to the earth. I mentioned it to another missionary working with the same people group who gave me some insight. He said, "It has something to do with their origins, perhaps their Indonesian background and homeland. I've also heard the mention of Mecca during these discussions." Maybe the east/west issue had something to do with the holy city of Islam, but what?

The Javanese were five or more generations removed from Indonesia when they were brought to Suriname as contract laborers. They were traditionally Muslims, although their heritage had large doses of Buddhism and Hinduism, with an overlay of traditional tribal religions. In Suriname they were collectively known as the people group that practiced Islam.

In Indonesia, when a Muslim faced Mecca for the five required daily prayer times, he did so by turning to the west, since that was the shortest distance. When the Javanese migrated to Suriname, someone determined that the shortest distance to Mecca was now accomplished by facing east. Before too long a controversy erupted in the Surinamese villages populated by these people. Those who turned their eyes to the east reasoned that their prayers would arrive in Mecca quicker than those who were facing west. The traditionalists argued that since their ancestors had always faced west, they were, therefore, forced to adhere to the old ways. The controversy continues to this day. And the final decision is made at one's funeral when the priest asks the men crowded around the open grave, "East or west?"

He's Beautiful!

After our first furlough, an additional role in government relations for the SIL branch took us out of the village as our primary residence. We were so grateful to find a 3-bedroom rented home on stilts in the capital city with a wrap-around balcony, one kilometer between the SIL office building and the American Cooperative School. We were also expecting our 2nd child!

Linda's Dutch lady doctor was with the Diaconessenziekenhuis, the Deaconesses' hospital, an institution with Moravian roots in the capital three kilometers from our home. There, white uniformed nurses with dark brown skin lined the hospital corridors to start each day singing a hymn that would echo down the hallways. Patient rooms were open to the outdoors with small balconies and no screens on the windows, lightweight cotton curtains pulled back to allow in the breeze. Some beds had mosquito netting. Mark was born at Diaconessenziekenhuis in the capital city of Paramaribo as was David.

My Mom was there for the occasion and Linda's parents would come later. When I announced a baby boy, David, now three-and-a-half, jumped up and down for joy. Oma was just as enthusiastic exclaiming in her Dutch accent, "He's *b-e-a-u-t-i-f-u-l!*" Linda decided early on it would be more comfortable at home enjoying our own balcony breeze with Oma there to help out rather than trying to get sleep in the hospital where mosquitoes freely roamed under beds and in corners. So after one sleepless night we were back home again with our second precious son.

Many hours were spent enjoying our breezy balcony. Palm branches rustled and coconuts grew at eye level from the towering trees that shot up from the saplings we planted. The boys' toys made their way out to the balcony too. Brightly colored Duplo would be strewn over the cool limestone tiles where they could simultaneously play and watch the happenings on the street below, diesel trucks puffing black smoke as they shifted at the intersection. After a while we discovered that a dining table placed on the balcony with a ceiling fan fixed above it made a wonderful spot to eat dinner midday rather than in the dining area of the kitchen where there was no breeze and a hot oven.

Other favorite spots were our screened-in bedrooms, windows wide open to the night sounds, listening to the distant rain make its way across the tin roofs until it pelted our own, or, Mom and Dad's bed in the middle of the afternoon, jalousie windows shut, the window air conditioner set to the coldest setting, and a read-aloud story in progress.

We would make trips back to Dessa to visit our Javanese friends and get caught up on the news. David and Mark disliked those excursions. As soon as we arrived, the older women would emerge from their humble dwellings and sidle up to them, 'kissing' them on their cheeks by sniffing, their mouths stained with the dark red juice of the betel nut.

Our home in the capital city, raised up on square concrete stilts, with the breezy wraparound balcony, tall royal palm trees, mango tree, ham radio antenna, and passion fruit vine on the trellis.

The hot cassava fries that magically appeared from their open kitchens made up for it.

As the boys grew older, most recreation was at the American Cooperative School where the missionary kids, the children of international businessmen, and kids from diplomats' families hung out. Cable TV arrived in Suriname at about this time. It seemed to change the simple lifestyle of many Surinamers. People gathered around their TV sets to watch the latest CNN broadcasts. Up until this time, Suriname was blessed with only two TV stations. The broadcasts started at 5:00 P.M. and ended at midnight or earlier, with mostly local content and some foreign. For the first 14 years, we had no TV and relied on shortwave radio for world news. But our boys spent their time outdoors, playing basketball and street hockey on the hard surface basketball court at the mission school. Great friendships were formed there as other fathers and their sons came out to play every Saturday morning or Sunday evening when the weather turned somewhat cooler. Many shoes were worn out on the rough surface of that court and the activities cemented us together as an expatriate community. Mark became a three-point shooter that no one could stop. He stood at the baseline, took careful aim, and swished the ball through the net almost every time.

BURN YOUR BED

This Language is Dying

I stared long and hard at the list of well-known names from the Javanese community. Twelve people had been handpicked by Suriname's Minister of Education to fix the spelling of Suriname Javanese once and for all. Many discussions had taken place over the years but none had resulted in a formal spelling (orthography) for this displaced Indonesian language spoken by 60,000 people. They were physically removed from their roots more than half a world away and more than a century removed chronologically.

I scanned the list again, noticing prominent church leaders, educators, government employees, and myself. It was 1986. We had done good research trying to figure out how the sound system worked phonemically, the foundation of a responsible orthography for the Suriname Javanese. The list contained only three people with any linguistic background, none of them Javanese: Dr. Eersel, a faculty member of the University of Suriname; Hein, a Dutch linguist, who had spent considerable years studying Javanese in Indonesia; and myself. With this formidable lineup I wasn't too hopeful that our suggested orthography would be adopted. I did feel, however, that our proposal had considerable professional merit and remained somewhat hopeful.

My thoughts turned to Dessa, where we witnessed daily the frustration experienced by Javanese schoolchildren trying to learn Dutch, a foreign language. The educational system required that all instruction be in Dutch, the formally adopted national language of this former Dutch colony. But what happened in the villages was a far cry from that formality. Five-year-old children went to school, never having spoken a word of Dutch, and now were expected to speak a language they didn't know or understand. How could anyone learn in that environment? Only the brightest ever passed the test upon leaving the sixth grade that served as a ticket to further learning. The teachers, likewise, were often unmotivated to instruct in the national language since it wasn't the first language for most of them either.

There were many days when Linda and I would peer out of our village abode, watching schoolchildren gleefully skip home along the narrow sandy roads, barely an hour after they had left to go to school. If the teacher didn't show up on a particular day, the students were sent home. If the bus carrying the teachers from the capital city to the village broke down, the entire village school day was canceled.

One hot and humid morning we looked out of our window to see thick black smoke filling the skies above the little three-room school, meant to house more than 100 children, grades 1 through 6. A propane cylinder in the school's kitchen had inexplicably exploded during the night, and the entire school burned down to the ground. The fire department didn't even show up, and parents were left to clean up the mess, retrieving whatever was left to salvage from the massive blaze.

Weeks went by before the village elders set up school in the recreational building next to the soccer field. But the small space was insufficient to house all of the students at once so they resorted to splitting the day into two. Grades 1-3 attended school in the morning and grades 4-6 followed in the afternoon. Without air-conditioning or even ceiling fans, learning was difficult in the tropical conditions of Suriname where the customary daytime temperature soared to the mid-90s year-round. High humidity added to the already miserable conditions. As soon as the rainy season began, the sandy roads turned to mud, making passage anywhere difficult. It was no wonder children frequently stayed home from school and formal learning stopped.

Wouldn't it make a lot more sense, I thought, *if education was conducted in the mother tongue of the students?* Instead of struggling with a foreign language when students began formal education, they would at least have a fighting chance to understand what the teacher was saying or trying to teach.

As Linda and I increased our languages skills in Suriname Javanese, I made a chart outlining language usage within the village. I divided the chart by gender, age, and occurrence. A clear and unmistakable pattern emerged from my investigation. Children, both boys and girls, spoke only Suriname Javanese up to the age of five or when they entered school, when they were required to learn Dutch, a foreign language. Teenagers quickly learned the country's lingua franca, known as Sranan Tongo, or Suriname Tongue, the creolized language of wider communication. They were proud to be able to speak this language because it gave them status among the other segments of the overall population. But there was no formal education in this language either. It was all oral. Adult males easily spoke Sranan Tongo because many of them worked in the capital city at day jobs that required them to have partially fluency in the language. Adult females preferred to speak Suriname Javanese, their mother tongue. Older men and women above 50 almost exclusively spoke Suriname Javanese. And yet Dutch was the national language. Linda and I were thrust into this mix, trying to understand it all and trying desperately to find a way that the spelling of the Suriname Javanese language could play into this.

The Spelling Commission was to last twelve weeks. There were only two proposals put forward, Hein's and ours. Hein's orthography was awkward because it used symbols that couldn't easily be reproduced on a typewriter, something extremely important to us for making future literacy books. But the Commission had a certain amount of faith in Hein because of the time he had spent in Indonesia. I had a Dutch background with little Indonesian experience, except for our four years spent in Dessa.

When I presented our proposed orthography, the Commission chairman, a pastor of a large Moravian church in Suriname, immediately began to make negative remarks about it. "Ed," he began, "I can assure you that in a few years, perhaps no more than a dozen, this language won't be spoken anymore in this country. The language is dying and all of our work will have been in vain. I was appointed to serve on this commission but I doubt that anything other than a formal statement will be the result of our efforts." His interest seemed to be in creating an internationally appealing orthography that would hold status, not a practical concern for the ease of learning by the average Suriname Javanese adult or child. The others seemed to agree with him and I started to feel like a loner, an outsider, wondering if my linguistic training had been sufficient. I went home discouraged and defeated after the second meeting. The common villager was being overlooked if we didn't use a simplified orthography.

I brought the matter up to our Wycliffe colleagues and they mounted a concerted prayer effort. That's when it hit me. What if I approached Dr. Eersel, the well-respected linguist and educator from the University and asked him to carry my proposal to the committee? We sat down over strong Dutch coffee in his cramped, disorganized office and I laid out our spelling proposal. I sensed that he was on board and understood the wider implications of our work. He respected the fact that we had come to Suriname to help the Javanese understand the Words of Life by having the Scriptures in their own language, not through a borrowed language nor through a language that was forced upon them.

When the committee reconvened, Dr. Eersel presented my proposal and the attention level of the group increased dramatically. It appeared as if the group was being swayed towards our proposal. Week after week, I fed Dr. Eersel more phonemic information about our orthography. When the commission concluded its work, they adopted our proposal, lock, stock, and barrel. Only one minor change had to be made but the spelling of Suriname Javanese was established. It was officially presented to the Minister of Education and later printed in the local newspapers. The predictions about the language dying out never materialized.

An Unmistakable Thud

In December 1989 I wanted to surprise Linda for Christmas by making an end table with inlaid Delft tiles for our living room. I promised her I would be back by lunchtime as the table saw was at the carpenter's shop five minutes away. The saw was outside, underneath a shelter with a tin roof. It occurred to me that it had been set up for a left-handed person, as our maintenance man was a southpaw, but I paid scant attention to it. It was baking underneath the shelter but I worked methodically, cutting the various pieces of lumber needed. I was ever so briefly distracted by a colleague who engaged me in a short conversation.

The next thing I knew I found myself lying on a makeshift bed in the emergency room of a third world hospital. I had just had a run-in with that saw, severing the index finger on my left hand. I had been lying there for 45 minutes when another colleague came running into the room holding a Ziploc bag filled with ice and the remains of my finger. He gave the bag to the Filipino intern who was attending my case. The doctor took the bag dripping with ice water, and dangled it in front of my eyes. My finger was clearly visible. He didn't say a word. He merely looked at me, shaking the bag all the while, waiting for my response. I thought, "What is he thinking? Surely he's not thinking that...?" My mind just would not go there.

I looked to my left at the equipment in the room. I observed the bed I was lying on, then glanced to my right and heard the person next to me screaming for attention. Finally I looked back at the doctor and stared into his eyes. Ever so slowly, I shook my head. The doctor reached over and dropped that little bag into the metal trash can next to my head. I heard it hit the bottom of the can with an unmistakable thud. "What in the world am I doing in this place, Lord? I've been in this country ten years with my wife and boys. I've missed many birthdays, Thanksgivings, holidays, and family outings the last ten years. Isn't ten years long enough? Is this worth it all?"

But the Lord didn't answer me that hot and muggy Saturday morning. No answers were forthcoming, not even a hint that I should do anything different. If I had the ability to look ten years into the future, I would have seen something I had not expected but had prayed for nonetheless. I would have seen myself sitting on the front row of the dedication of the New Testament in the Suriname Javanese language. I would have seen myself, Antoon, his wife Wanda, and Linda, in a huge hall as the guests of honor, with hundreds of Javanese giving glory to God, and thanking Him for the completed Scriptures in their own language. These Javanese had come to know Jesus as their Messiah since we arrived twenty years ago.

But I was unable to look into the future. I was in that emergency ward and my finger was chopped off. I had to believe that God was fully in charge, didn't make mistakes, and knew exactly what was on my mind at that moment. It would be a moment I would recall frequently, serving as a poignant reminder that perseverance eventually bears fruit. There would be additional opportunities to reinforce that powerful notion in the not-too-distant future.

A White Man's Religion

Paidie, a Suriname Javanese Muslim, came home from his job as a night watchman one October morning in 1993. As he climbed into bed he glanced over to the nightstand. Something was not quite right. Next to the lamp was a book he had never seen before. He read the title, "Dongèngané Markus", the Gospel of Mark. Several years earlier, Antoon had translated it and copies had been available for about ten years. Parmi, Paidie's wife, who had been attending one of the new church plants, purchased the publication and brought it home. Paidie was an avid reader in Dutch. He picked up the booklet and for the first time in his life, read something in his native language. Seeing the Suriname Javanese publication challenged an assumption he had all of his life: *Christianity is a white man's religion.* That evening he would take the booklet to work.

As Paidie was preparing to go to bed that morning, he did something he had done for more than 20 years. He tucked a Dutch Bible underneath his pillow and slept on it, a ritual of sorts. When he went to work that evening, he took that Gospel of Mark and stuffed it in his shirt. His co-workers were also Muslims, and he would be ostracized if found carrying Christian literature. He wanted to find out if there was any truth to this white man's religion. He put his Dutch Bible into his satchel, and would compare it to the Suriname Javanese, to make absolutely sure they agreed.

He and his colleagues settled into the monotonous routine of guarding government buildings. At three o'clock in the morning when all good night watchmen fall asleep, he grabbed a couple of rickety wooden chairs, sat down on one and propped his feet up on the other, underneath a faint fluorescent bulb. Glancing at his colleagues to make sure they were indeed asleep, he pulled the little booklet out of his shirt. Next he took out his Dutch Bible, and opened it to Mark chapter 1. As he read the Suriname Javanese portion, he compared it to the Dutch. He read through chapters one, two, and three. When he got to chapter four, he set aside the Dutch Bible, convinced that the portions in Javanese had been faithfully translated. He read all sixteen chapters of the Gospel of Mark that night and was spellbound. This was challenging him.

In the morning he went home, saw Parmi just before she went off to her pharmacy job and asked her if she could find any more Bible portions in the language. She said, "I've heard that they were working on Paul's Letters. I'll see if I can find a copy." Paidie went off to bed, tucking the Dutch Bible underneath his pillow.

Eventually Parmi returned with another booklet containing Paul's letters to the Galatians, Ephesians, Philippians, and Colossians. She laid that on his nightstand. The following evening Paidie took the new booklet, stuffed that into his shirt and marched off to work, leaving his Dutch Bible at home. At three o'clock, when all good night watchmen fall asleep, he grabbed those wooden chairs, sat down, propped his feet up and started to read the words of life. He read through Galatians, Ephesians, and then Philippians. When he got to Philippians Chapter 3 verse 10, he read these powerful words, "...*supaya ya aku bias kenal marang Dèkné lan ngrasakké kawasané...*" (I want to know Christ—yes, to know the power of his resurrection and participation in his sufferings, becoming like him in his death.) Paidie was stunned by these powerful words. "Do you mean to say that I can know Christ?" he whispered to himself, "is it possible to know Christ?" And an arrow went through Paidie's heart. He got up from his chair, turned around and entered a small room where the night watchmen kept their day clothes, closed the door, got on his knees and prayed a simple prayer. "God, are you telling me that I can know You, the God of the universe? Oh, I want to know this God." When he got up, something was different. He was a new man.

Paidie was aware that the translation of the New Testament in his language was in full swing. He set out on a search and found me sitting in my office at the Translation Center in Paramaribo. "Ed, I love my language, and I love my people. Is there something I can do to help?"

Paidie became our literacy expert. I rearranged the small 10' x 10' office to make space for him and Linda to work on the literacy material, beginning with the first syllable in the Suriname Javanese primer. The timing was impeccable. David, and now Mark, were both in school during the day until one o'clock, freeing up Linda to join me in the office. In a short time, Paidie was writing the stories that would become the basis for teaching his people to read and write. He and Linda worked tirelessly for many years, producing all the primers and booklets needed for a complete literacy program.

BURN YOUR BED

Max

"Oh, no! Honey, we've been robbed. I can't believe it's happened again," I yelled at Linda as I ran downstairs to the car, its doors were swung wide. As I surveyed the damage, I felt a pit in the bottom of my stomach. The radio, the newly installed after-market CD player, speakers, woofer, and equalizer, everything…gone in a flash. When I reported the theft to the police, asking them to come, they said that they didn't have a vehicle available and so I picked them up. The police took down all the pertinent information and suggested I get a guard dog. We hesitated getting a dog because it meant finding someone to care for it during furloughs. Canned or prepared dog food was not widely available. We would have to cook rice for a dog, along with scrap meat from the butcher that had an obnoxious odor.

Since moving to the city several years earlier, we had been robbed seven times. Once, we unfortunately left our plastic Adirondacks sitting outside on the upstairs balcony. Linda and I had been out on a date and when we returned and walked upstairs, we saw the now-empty space. A petty thief had climbed over the gate, came up the outside concrete steps, grabbed the four chairs and walked off down the road, completely ignored and unnoticed by anyone. Perhaps it was the same opportunist that had come knocking on our gate the week before. The metallic clanging meant there was someone at the gate. As I walked down to meet him, he held out his hand, asking for money. We were not in the habit of giving money to beggars but were willing to give food. He walked away with a plastic bag full of warm rice and vegetables, leftovers from supper. He looked at me rather disgruntled, turned, and walked away. As he ambled down the bricked street, he tossed something into the ditch. I bicycled to the spot and found the bag lying there. At least the rats had something to eat.

On another occasion, we came home late and realized a small-time thief had climbed over the gate and helped himself to the laundry hanging on the clothes lines suspended beneath the house. He had methodically searched out the male clothing that fit him and took off with his treasure. We told ourselves we would not be forced to learn that lesson twice.

After seven robberies, our colleagues pleaded with us to get a good guard dog and we finally relented and got two. Max and Sox were from the same litter. When they were approximately six weeks old, we brought them home. These Brazilian Filas would grow to about 40 lb. and 20 inches in height. Max looked like a small Lab, with liquid eyes and drooping ears. Sox was black with white paws. David adopted Sox and Mark got Max. During the first few weeks, both dogs developed distemper. Linda fed them with an eye dropper and nursed them back to health but Sox succumbed the second time he contracted the debilitating disease. David, 11, was distraught. "Come on Dave," I said, "let's give Sox a proper burial." We wrapped the still warm, now lifeless body into a black plastic bag and dug a hole in the back corner of the yard. David gently placed his canine friend into the two-foot deep hole and said good-bye to Sox. We erected a small wooden cross over the mound of dirt. It was a tearful end to a faithful friend. Max would have to carry on without his sibling.

Whenever someone knocked on our gate, Max would run out and bark incessantly, defiantly displaying his sharp teeth. Frequently he would nip at their clothing through the barred gate. One of the boys would have to fetch Max and tie him up so that our guests could come inside. Our house sat on square concrete stilts to catch the tropical breeze and stay above the mosquitoes that came out during rush hour, a period of time a half hour before sunset and lasting for about half an hour after sunset. We were only 6° north of the equator in this tropical country and daylight hours varied by no more than 30 minutes from the day with the shortest daylight hours to the longest. The boys didn't need watches. They knew they had to be home by sunset. It was easy.

Max slept in the sandbox beneath the outdoor wooden staircase. No one in this tropical country kept their dogs inside. With an annual average daytime temperature of 95°F and average nighttime temperature of 80°F, there was no reason for anyone or anything to be cold.

It was still daylight when the boys came home, parking their bikes under the house. Max was roaming there, providing protection. David and Mark were proud of their bikes. We had gone to great lengths to secure them and they rode their two-wheeled treasures everywhere. When a friend showed up, we put Max on his leash to let him in. As Benji prepared to go home, we unleashed the dog and David let out a yell, "Dad, someone stole our bikes!" A thief had come into the yard in broad daylight, noticed that the dog was tied up and taken the boys' bicycles. At suppertime we committed it to the Lord and asked him to help us find the bikes. In this country where everyone and his brother owned a bike as a necessary form of transportation, it would take a miracle to recover their two-wheeled steeds.

We had recorded the serial numbers of all of our bikes in case of theft. Now we were ready. Night after night we prayed. I put a glass jar with some turpentine and a rag in the car. We reasoned that whoever stole the bikes would probably spray paint them to disguise them. The rag and turpentine would come in handy to reveal the true identity of the bikes should we find them.

A few days later, we heard the familiar clanging of the gate. It was John, our SIL colleague. He had been to the Chinese store down the street and noticed a group of teenage boys standing there with their bikes. John recognized both of our boys' bikes, grabbed Mark's and threw it into the back of his pickup. But the group of young hooligans quickly mounted the remaining bikes and pedaled off before he could catch them. One down, one to go. Thank you, Lord.

On a Saturday afternoon, about a week later, we were at a nearby outdoor sports complex when David noticed a young boy pedal past. "Dad," he yelled under his breath, "that's my bike!" "Are you sure?" I said. "There are hundreds of bikes around here. Make sure you take another look." The boy was riding a silver colored bike. David's was originally black with neon green forks, but the unmistakable tear in the banana-shaped seat was the telltale sign. The unsuspecting boy rode by once more. We quietly stepped in front of him, trying to avoid drawing the attention to the others playing soccer on the various fields. He quickly dismounted. I hurriedly walked to the car to retrieve the rag and turpentine. When I rubbed off the fresh paint, the silver fell away revealing the bike's original black. The neon green forks, however, had not been repainted. The serial number matched ours exactly. I asked the boy where he had obtained the bike and he mumbled something about a cousin giving it to him. "Come on," I offered, "let's go down to the police station and settle this." The boy turned and ran off as fast as he could. We had both of our bikes back. At suppertime, we rejoiced over the Lord's excellent provision.

A few weeks later I woke up to Max's incessant barking at 2:30 A.M. Why is that dog barking in the middle of the night? I quickly got dressed and quietly opened the back door leading to the outside steps. Max was furiously nipping at someone's heels who had climbed over the fence and inadvertently walked right into the sandbox where Max slept. The stranger was carrying a large bag, ready to plunder whatever he could from underneath our raised house. I slowly made my way down the stairs and then I started to laugh. A typical David and Goliath scene was unfolding. A 40 lb. dog was holding a 200 lb. man at bay. The thief tried to turn and run but Max just kept nipping at his heels. Ever so slowly, he turned towards Max and started to back out towards the gate. Max was relentless in his pursuit. The would-be thief was swinging his empty bag, trying to fend off this ferocious canine but Max kept at the unwelcome stranger. When he got to the gate, he swung one leg over it but his pant leg got caught. He fell onto the driveway on the other side of gate, safely out of the harm's way from Max. He hightailed it down the road, with Max barking in delight. "Who needs a dog?" I remember saying to my friends. Who indeed?

Mark and David giving Max his weekly shampoo and bath

BURN YOUR BED

Prove God Strong

On a Friday afternoon in late July 1989, I received a phone call that would have an unforeseen impact on me. Nick, a Wycliffe colleague, was on the line. "Ed," he started, "we have a staffing shortage here in British Columbia. We were expecting some of our furloughing staff to teach the September course but due to a family tragedy, they won't be able to make it. Would you and Linda considering coming out west from Michigan for the month to fill the gap?" I glanced at our calendar. Our furlough appointments for August were made, speaking here and there. September wasn't looking any better. "It doesn't look promising Nick," I said in reply. "Ok," Nick said, "I'll call again on Monday to find out what your answer is. We need someone to teach that course in September."

I prayed silently asking the Lord what we were supposed to do. This seemed like an impossible request. We had arranged all of our fall speaking engagements and it wouldn't be easy to change them. Furlough only comes around once every three or four years. It's a frantic time of visiting and reporting to all of one's prayer and financial partners, and each and every visit is a treasured one. Now we were being asked to consider helping our colleagues in British Columbia. What was it that God wanted us to do? I had never even taught a Sunday School class, and the thought of standing in front of the classroom terrified me. I reasoned that God was not asking me to do this. My mind engaged in an unwinnable battle.

As the weekend wore on, the answers were not forthcoming. Saturday morning came and went. Nothing. Saturday afternoon and evening came and went. Still nothing. On Sunday morning we went to church but we didn't hear God's voice speaking to us about the next day's phone call. We were in a quandary. Nick would be calling in the morning and I still had no answer. Prayer did not come easy. In the middle of the afternoon the phone rang. It was Lynne, Linda's longtime girlfriend. "Would you and Ed like to come to church with me this evening? I think you'll really enjoy our pastor's teaching."

"Please finish this sentence," the pastor said. "Water always seeks the path…" In unison we said, "…of least resistance." "That's right." he said, "Water is lazy and for the most part, so are we. Some of you are at a crossroads and don't know which way to turn. You're at a fork in the road. If you turn one way, you'll be choosing the easy way out. If you turn the other way, you'll see only impossible challenges ahead. I challenge you to choose the road with the greater resistance. I want you to prove God strong." The pastor's eyes seemed to bore a hole right through me. How did he know that I was at that exact point? I didn't hear the rest of the message but I already knew what my answer would be when Nick called the following morning.

As a college sophomore, I remember signing up for Golf 101 during the fall semester. I had never golfed but was eager to learn. On Monday morning when the first class session convened, twenty five students showed up. The P.E. instructor looked out over the mostly male classroom and said, "I have taught this course many times. From previous experience, I know that some of you are already well acquainted with the game. This course is not for you. This course is for beginners. If you're here because you think you can squeeze out an easy grade for yourself, let me assure you that won't happen. Let me repeat, if you've had a substantial amount of golf in your past, this course is not for you. I'll know soon enough who you are. If so, then your grade will be an automatic 'F'," he concluded. On Wednesday morning when the class reconvened, twelve students showed up, proving the instructor's point.

Meanwhile, we made our way to British Columbia. I conveyed my hesitancy to the staff that I had no teaching experience and would need every one of their daily prayers. The thought of standing up in front of a class and teaching for an hour seemed unthinkable. The staff reassured me, however, that they had all been in the same position at one time or another. If I had known that years later I would thrive here, I would have believed that they were talking to someone else.

The month passed quickly. The staff surrounded me with their prayers and support and each new day became an adventure of its own. Within days I found that, to my great joy, I came to life as I taught the classes I had fretted about only a few days earlier. By the time the month had passed, I was already inquiring about the possibility of returning the following year for a repeat performance.

For several years we returned to Canada or the US to teach at the one-month course. These became wonderful opportunities to play into the lives of the new members entering the Wycliffe organization.

Proving God strong became a habit. After we left Suriname, we jumped at the chances to lead short term Wycliffe trips around the world. We were continually amazed how small steps of obedience always led to huge blessings. At no point in time, however, was that more evident than when we were under duress or spiritual attack.

BURN YOUR BED

The Sandford Files

Something marvelous took place that fall as we taught in British Columbia. I gained a confidence like I had not had before. We made our way back to Suriname after our furlough and hit the ground running, churning out book after New Testament book. It was as if Antoon had been waiting for this all of his life but didn't realize it. At Christmastime I had my hand accident but quickly recovered. Then in January something even more wonderful took place. Several of our colleagues had been talking about getting together to do an in-home Bible study. We eagerly offered our home for the Sunday evening meetings. We chose to read and study a book that was making significant inroads in the world of Christianity, *The Transformation of the Inner Man* by John and Paula Sandford.

Week after week we studied this insightful publication in light of the Scriptures. During the following months, we dug into the Word, verifying the writings of this husband and wife team. A chapter entitled <u>Bitter Root Judgment and Expectancy</u> grabbed my attention as few things ever have. There, I read about the dangers of hanging onto unforgiveness and started contemplating this truth in my own life.

I had been told that the Javanese were experts at holding grudges. When we lived in the village during those initial four years, we learned about that firsthand. Whenever someone was building a new house or doing some construction, it was expected that any eligible male would come to help lay the foundation to help get things off to a good start, an event that I regularly took part in. But frequently I was unable to help due to circumstances beyond my control.

One specific neighbor seemed miffed at my inability to help him for more than one day. In this close-knit community, news (and gossip) spread like wildfire. When the time came for us to build a small carport next to our house, I was afraid no one would come to help us, but half a dozen men showed up with their shovels to help mix the cement, with the exception of that one neighbor. It was backbreaking work since everything was done manually. All day long we worked in the blistering sun, mixing and shoveling cement until we were finally done. The neighbor in mention had passed by a few times, eyeing me carefully but never acknowledging me. For the remainder of our time in the village, about two years, I was unable to determine if he was genuinely upset with me or just really enjoyed holding a grudge. I asked Antoon about it and he reassured me that the Javanese were the world's specialists at holding grudges. It does make me wonder, from time to time, what there is in our culture that we're good at concealing, or not willing to deal with. Probably lots.

One hot and humid afternoon, Antoon and I were sitting in our translation center, discussing some problems with the translation of the Book of John. After half an hour, a colleague working on a translation in another language, walked by. He said, "Ed, can I see you a minute?" I excused myself and walked just far enough, or so I thought, that Antoon couldn't hear us. My colleague said, "I want to apologize for what happened the other day. I was wrong." I knew what he was talking about and I reassured him of my forgiveness. As far as I was concerned, the matter was over. The exchange was short, lasting less than a minute. But it was an important minute because it kept the communication channels open and our hearts attuned to God's will and Spirit. I walked back to the table where Antoon was sitting, hoping to resume our discussion about the issues in the Gospel of John. But it wasn't going to happen. Antoon turned to me and with a compassionate and jealous look in his eye said, "Ed, I wish my people would learn to do that!"

Back at the Bible study, nagging thoughts of my father continued to plague me. I could feel the bitterness rise up inside me, just recalling the incidents of my youth. I wondered how that was feeding into my mind. Was my Dad still influencing my behavior, even though he was thousands of miles away? In spite of the fact that I hadn't seen him in over a dozen years, I couldn't deny the fact that his presence was somehow still felt. For weeks we studied the principles of forgiveness and consequences of unforgiveness. I knew something had to be done and as we prayed and studied, it finally became clear: I had to forgive my father for all he had said and done and maybe more importantly, I had to forgive myself. This was not going to be easy. I struggled with it for weeks. The longer I waited and struggled, the harder it became. Freedom was within my grasp but I kept thinking about all the times that Dad had called my siblings and me 'big zeroes'. Had he really meant that or was he just talking out of frustration in not seeing his own potential realized? Was he really as bad as he appeared? Was he just the product of parents who didn't know how to love on their son, or great-grandparents who didn't know how to love on their children? Regardless, I knew something had to be done and it had to be done quickly. I determined that now was the perfect opportunity and that if I didn't act now, the chance might never return.

The following week I plunged in with both feet, not waiting for the prayer time which usually ended the evening's study. I got on my knees and my colleagues came around me, holding me up. I sobbed like a baby, telling the Lord that I was forgiving my father for all the negative things he had said to me for all those years. I told God I was forgiving myself for believing all those lies I had been told or had been telling myself. It was as if scales fell off my eyes. My colleagues rejoiced over the lifting of this heavy burden. A huge weight lifted off my shoulders. I was free!

But it didn't culminate there. Over the past several years, I had let my devotional time slip, arguing with myself that translating the word of God was probably a reasonable substitute for having a daily devotion. Was I ever wrong on that score! Translating God's word was quite insightful and rewarding in terms of Biblical knowledge but it can also be an academic exercise. In fact, I have come to the conclusion that translation is largely an academic exercise; one needs to employ good linguistic practices to do it well. No, I couldn't be using the job of Bible translation as a substitute for my walk with God. And I determined that I was going to be spending a lot more personal time digging into the Book of Books for my own spiritual growth.

At the same time, I was starting to notice that my clothes weren't fitting as well as they used to. I was punching extra holes in my belts and my knees were starting to ache as a result of the extra pounds I was carrying. A colleague invited us to join him and his wife for a brisk, pre-dawn walk. Within days, Linda and I decided that getting 30 minutes of exercise a day would become a lifetime habit, a decision we have yet to regret.

Uncannily around the same time, I received a phone call from Canada. It was my father! He called to let me know that he had a gift for me. I hadn't heard his voice or seen him in more than 20 years. He didn't let me know what the gift was. I was skeptical at first but decided that I need not be scared or frightened. After all, I had dealt with it. But was I ready for a face-to-face encounter after almost two decades? I wasn't convinced but prayed about it.

The meeting place and time was established. Part of our furlough would be spent in Canada. I was nervous. How would I act? How would my Dad react to seeing ours sons, ages 15 and 12, for the first time? In July of 1996 we met at a restaurant along Highway 401, near London. My father greeted us and David and Mark. The meeting was friendly but contrived. My father was still the same person I had remembered so many years earlier. It was a colossal disappointment but I had faced the giant and it was no longer a huge albatross around my neck. The big surprise turned out to be his decision to return a few photographs that he had taken with him during his rushed exit twenty-two years earlier. One of those photographs appears in this book on page 22. The others were of my growing up years. My decision to forgive my father during the Bible Study had proven to be one of the biggest and best decisions of my life. The monkey was off my back and I was grateful for the way I had faced my father after all those years without fear, judgment, or retribution. Within two years, my father's life on earth would be over, a brain aneurysm claiming his life.

The Ambassadors

I walked up the massive, red carpeted sweeping staircase and was met by the Soviet ambassador extending a plateful of typical Russian delicacies. "Caviar, Mr. Speyers?" he asked. He helped himself to another generous portion and offered me the same. "Mr. Speyers, tell me again, what is your true purpose in Suriname and why have you honored me by coming for a visit to our embassy?" The ambassador suspiciously eyed my briefcase, and pointing to it he said, "Do you mind if we have a look inside your satchel, please?" A quick search revealed several literacy books produced by our Wycliffe colleagues, which I gladly left behind for the graying statesman. I had come to the Soviet Embassy at the invitation of Stasis Obukauskas, the second secretary and consul whom I had met earlier that month at a diplomatic party, in my role as government relations officer for SIL in Suriname.

In 1983 our Government Relations officer returned to the Netherlands and the branch asked me to resume his responsibilities, which I did through 1989. Serving as the GR officer for our branch would include visits to many diplomatic offices, both foreign and domestic, and securing permanent visas, residency permits, tax clearances, etc., for our 30+ members.

Mr. Obukauskas served in Suriname for 2½ years before he was brutally shot to death along the highway leading to the international airport. No one claimed responsibility and the embassy remained silent about the whole affair. The following day, however, three Surinamers were arrested in connection with the attempted robbery and subsequent murder. When the Soviet Union broke up in 1991, their embassy went up for sale and a local group bought the building, converting it to the Residence Inn. Ironically, well over half of the guests that came for the dedication of the Suriname Javanese Scriptures years later, stayed there, enjoying the sumptuous surroundings, along with that massive sweeping staircase and grand chandeliers that were still in place. Our invited guests insisted that Linda and I stay in the room that used to be the ambassador's personal luxury suite. Gold-plated doorknobs, handles, and faucets were everywhere. How ironic I thought, that a building I once visited to gain favor with Soviet diplomats had now become my bedroom. I couldn't help but smile glancing at the luxurious environs.

During the time of my role in Government Relations, the military continued to tighten its grip on the reins of power, the Dutch embassy also came under fire. The Surinamese government demanded that millions of dollars be released from the Netherlands for economic development, funds that Suriname claimed the Netherlands had promised to them after she declared her independence in 1975. When the brutal political murders of December 1982 occurred, the Netherlands decided to withhold those funds in protest. I had become acquainted with the Dutch ambassador, because several of our translators were from the Netherlands and I invited him to come and visit the translation center and meet our Dutch colleagues. Our friendship grew and I made frequent visits to the Dutch Embassy, reassuring him that our people were doing good linguistic work in the country's languages.

He was into computers and we eagerly traded computing tips. He had two golden retrievers that were not used to the heat and humidity of this little country next to the equator. More than once, when the air-conditioning system failed in the ambassador's residence, his wife called KLM, the major Dutch air carrier, to arrange for a quick trip back to Amsterdam to find relief for her suffering dogs. Years earlier, the same ambassador had been the major emissary for the Netherlands to Japan. During his tenure there, he brokered a deal between KLM and the Japanese government to initiate a new route, Schiphol to Tokyo. As a reward, the airline offered the ambassador free flights within KLM's world.

The Surinamese government eventually requested the Dutch dignitary be withdrawn due to a political confrontation. When we heard the news, I made my way to the Dutch embassy to meet one last time with him. Upon leaving, he graciously invited Linda and me to an exclusive farewell dinner that would be hosted in one of Suriname's finer waterfront homes, the Corner House. The extravagant affair was a bittersweet moment. Linda and I, along with a dozen other invited guests, sat through the dinner quite star-gazed by the opulent occasion. White-coated servants carried plates full of delicious local and international food and treats. We sat in absolute wonder that evening. How was it possible that we ordinary working linguists could participate in such a fabulous happening? Several years later, we would enjoy lunch with the ambassador and his wife at their home in the Netherlands.

In 1987, the leader of a ragtag group of a dozen men with guns and knives known as the Jungle Commandos, an anti-military faction, seized a Mission Aviation Fellowship (MAF) pilot, Dan Rogers, and his single-engine Cessna, when Dan made a flight into Djoemoe deep in Suriname's interior. The leader of the group, Ronnie Brunswijk, asked Dan to teach him how to fly. Ronnie had sinister plans to use the airplane to drop gasoline-filled barrels as homemade bombs on army installations. Linda and I had heard about Dan's capture and we made our way to their home in the capital city, where we found Sylvia, his wife, hovering nervously near the shortwave radio for any latest news.

After 9 or 10 instructional flights, Dan was released unharmed and made his way back to Paramaribo via French Guiana, the country directly to Suriname's east. The first time Mr. Brunswijk started the engine of the Cessna 206 to make his solo flight would also be his last. He attempted to land but crashed in doing so, leaving the precious airplane on the airstrip. Earlier, the commando leader had spray painted the 6-seater aircraft with green leopard spots all over its aluminum skin.

MAF was not content to leave the now-disabled bird in the jungle and asked Terry Hibbs, an MAF pilot who had earlier served in Suriname, to evaluate the condition of the plane. Terry flew to Suriname. Political conditions had deteriorated to the point where almost no one was allowed into the jungle areas. He would have to gain entry to the interior by going through French Guiana and then hop across the border back into Suriname. Terry would need a visa to French Guiana.

A year earlier, Linda and I had met a young couple with the French Embassy. Nettie, a Dutch woman and her husband Franck, the attaché at the French Embassy. We had become good friends and they were frequent guests in our home on Jerrystraat in Paramaribo. When I mentioned to Franck the situation regarding Terry needing a visa for French Guiana to evaluate the condition of MAF's plane, Franck said, "Let me talk to the ambassador." A few days later Terry had his visa in hand for French Guiana, thanks to Franck's good work. Terry went to French Guiana, made his way down the Marowijne River and hopped into Suriname, a roundabout way to gain entry to the crippled aircraft. He spent several days taking the wings off the plane and securing two large dugout canoes. He made a platform for the fuselage to rest on and secured the wings to the sides of the fuselage. It must have been quite a sight to see the white with red stripes, green polka-dotted Cessna balanced on top of the platform, which in turn, was perched on top of the two canoes, floating downstream to the resort town of Albina. A few days later, Terry returned to Paramaribo with the airplane on the back of a large truck and delivered it to the MAF hangar. Eventually a repair team came down and completely restored the once damaged aircraft. It went back into service ferrying people and goods into the jungle, all for God's glory.

Before my years as GR officer while we lived in Dessa, we invited the Indonesian ambassador and his wife to our village. I can still remember the dignitary's black limousine driving over the little bridge that Buck and I had built a year earlier. The ambassador and his wife deftly stepped out and we escorted them to the garage-like shelter I had built next to the house. When we greeted them in Suriname Javanese, they smiled broadly, nodding their approval. We explained to the ambassador that the 60,000 Suriname Javanese needed to have a translation of God's Word in their own language. Outside linguistic pressure had caused it to become its own language. It too, would need its own version of the Scriptures. The ambassador, a Muslim, smiled in agreement. A later visit to the ornate Indonesian Embassy proved beneficial. They ordered a large number of our literacy booklets and asked how a literacy program could be started to help the Suriname Javanese become increasingly bilingual. We had done our homework and were ready with a plethora of booklets designed for the purpose.

Watching the Super Bowl was not something any of us ex-patriates could even dream about. The very idea brought a high level of excitement to our fellowship. None of us owned a satellite dish, especially one large enough to pick up the signals from a geo-stationary satellite flung into outer space 25,000 miles away. But the U.S. Embassy did. We could see the dish-shaped structure standing inside their walled fortress. It was some 25 feet in diameter, unmistakable in its appearance.

Starting in the early 1990s, the expatriate community was invited to the embassy by the ambassador to come and watch the Super Bowl. We were scanned, badged, and ushered to the 5th floor of the imposing building, located on a major street in the capital city. The embassy reminded us of an American office building. It was the strangest of feelings when we left and drove to our homes, on the left hand side of the road, through the all-encompassing heat and humidity. We had been transported to America for a few short hours, and it was difficult to wrap our heads around it.

I was a frequent visitor to the embassy, registering our US workers, and I soon became acquainted with the ambassador. When I thanked him for having us over to watch the Super Bowl, he asked me if I wanted to watch videos of Monday Night Football games as well. From then on, every Tuesday morning starting the next fall, a chauffeur from the embassy drove up to our city home and personally delivered a video tape of Monday night's game, which David, Mark, and I would watch the same evening. This went on for about two years and when that ambassador left for his new assignment, the newly appointed dignitary continued the tradition.

The American ambassador was a great sports enthusiast and enjoyed biking and running. His children attended the missionary kids' school, the American Cooperative School. We competed together in the Annual Sports Day held at the school. I invited him to our translation center so that he could see for himself what our little expatriate community was accomplishing among the language groups in Suriname. He knew about SIL in other countries where he had served for the State Department and continued to be impressed with our motivation and dedication.

In 1999, when we finished with the translation of the Suriname Javanese New Testament, he was invited, along with his wife and other local dignitaries to attend the ceremony. The 50 guests we had personally invited from Canada and the US were in for a secret treat during their five-day stay. I had arranged with the ambassador to have our group for lunch at his personal residence which overlooked the Suriname River. When we boarded the bus for his residence I announced the news to the group. They were wild with excitement as most of the group had never met an ambassador or any diplomat from a country's state department.

The bus rolled up to his palatial gated residence, and the guard opened the electrically operated gate to allow us entry. The statesman greeted us as we stepped off the bus and invited us to tour the grounds of this tax-payer funded property. Off in the distance, dolphins could be seen jumping in the Suriname River. The entire scene was impressive to say the least, and the outdoor luncheon was no less so. Linda and I often felt that living in Suriname was like being a large fish in a small fishbowl.

But the best ambassadors we ever entertained in Suriname weren't ambassadors at all, not in the formal sense of the word. This couple were ambassadors from God. Ken and June had been friends for many years, who made it their ministry to be friends to missionaries. They knew and supported over 50 missionaries when we got to know them. We first met them before we ever set foot in this tropical country.

On a Sunday afternoon in the summer of 1978 in Michigan, Linda and I were invited to attend a new church. We were at a low point in our fund raising activities and we reluctantly joined Linda's girlfriend in Grand Rapids that sultry afternoon. The pastor gave an unforgettable sermon that evening from the Book of The Revelation, chapter 3.

After the service, we were standing in the narthex milling around the crowd when a man of short stature came up and stuck his hand out. He said, "Hi. I'm Ken. Who are you?" I stammered that we were visiting from another church and were missionaries with Wycliffe Bible Translators, preparing for the field. He said, "Oh, June and I love missionaries. I want you to meet my wife." He called her over, "June, come over here. I want you to meet this great couple. They're going to go to Suriname to translate the Bible for the Suriname Javanese people." She glanced over to her husband who was clearly enjoying himself by now and said, "OK honey. I'll be with you in a moment." Without a second glance or even giving me a chance to respond, Ken turned to me said, "June and I are going to support you two every year, starting now." I couldn't believe what I was hearing. Here was a man whom I had met just five minutes ago telling me that he was going to be a major supporter and I hadn't even had the opportunity to tell him much about our work, background, or future plans. I was floored. I stared at him and stammered, "Are you talking about this church?" "No, no, no. Nothing of the sort," Ken said, "I'm talking about June and myself. We want to be a part of your ministry starting now. I'll arrange to have the church involved separately. They'll participate in your Bible translation work as well." My mind was reeling from all this good news. God had prepared us to be at this place at this time.

Ken and June became close friends and we invited them to Suriname. We had been on the field about five years when they made a visit culminating in a tour of our Translation Center. Ken was clearly disturbed by the lack of air-conditioning in the building. The offices only had ceiling fans. A short while later, a check arrived in the mail that was large enough to air-condition every last office in the building. The branch ordered enough units for each of the offices. Life would never be the same again in that building. Sometimes the Lord sends friends who have a true heart for knowing needs and meeting them. There were ambassadors and then there were ambassadors.

BURN YOUR BED

Stop Signs and Molotov Cocktails

L inda was working in the kitchen when she heard the unmistakable sound of screeching tires and crunching metal. As she turned to see the action, she witnessed a car slamming into another at the intersection. Our home was located right on a corner in the capital city for the 15 years following our first term in the village. We observed that it was normal to ignore the stop and yield signs. The car had crashed into the stop sign, obliterating it, flipped over on its roof and skidded to a stop a hundred feet down the brick-paved road. A woman emerged from the upturned vehicle visibly shaken but unharmed. By the time I got home from the office, the wreckage had been towed away but the intersection was without signage in two directions.

My nightly routine consisted of pedaling home from the office just before dark, putting my feet up, a cool drink in hand, and enjoying the tropical breeze that drifted across our spacious balcony. Night after night I would sit there just prior to a light evening supper and gaze in amazement and wonder at the sight before me. Tall royal palm trees swayed in the evening breeze, growing taller by the day. We had planted them a few years earlier as seedlings and they had grown to a height of fifty feet. Bougainvillea bushes and colorful flamboyant trees spread their branches and beauty everywhere. The fragrant smell of the passion fruit vine we had planted was intoxicating.

The large mango tree, dripping with delicious fruit that magically appeared twice each year, was an eager enticement for any young boy who happened by. The only barrier was the property's fence, but frequently, even that was not enough of a deterrent. David and Mark loved to climb that tree. David fell out of it once and broke his right arm. Mark fell out of the jungle gym at the school and broke his arm and David also broke his left arm at school. We got to know our way around the hospital to the emergency room. Those visits would cost us about $5 every time we went. We were thankful for at least basic medical care.

A sudden burst of rain coming through the neighborhood, would send me scampering from my second floor balcony perch. We loved hearing the frequent tropical rainstorms making their way through the area, striking the galvanized tin roofs with such force that it drowned out all conversation. But what intrigued me the most was the total disregard for the stop and yield signs at the corner. We witnessed accident after near accident from our tiled L-shaped balcony. Now, with the stop signs lying in the overgrown ditch, I wondered how long it would take before they would be repaired or replaced. I should have known the answer because many other intersections in the neighborhood had suffered a similar fate. I finally determined to do something about it.

Well before dawn one Saturday morning, I walked over to the intersection and pulled one of the broken signs out of the tall snarling weeds. I went to the other corner and pulled that sign out of the tangled vines. Both wooden poles had snapped upon impact with vehicles. I carried them to the house and placed them on the empty 55-gallon drums stored there. I acquired two galvanized poles, each about 10 feet long, removed the old signs from their wooden perches and cleaned them up as best I could. Then I went to work repainting the now-weathered signage to replicate their former days. Stops signs in Suriname are round, with a red inverted triangle clearly displayed across the face of the sign. The word "STOP" is emblazoned over top of that triangle, all on a white background. I would need some red, black, and white outdoor paint to start the job and some hardware to complete it.

Over the next two or three Saturdays, I worked diligently securing all the parts and paint and finishing the job a few weeks later. Cars kept having minor incidents at the corner but it was predictable that most accidents occurred at intersections. It became a sport for our family to have dinner on the balcony and watch the hits and near misses on an almost daily basis.

Early one morning, to avoid the inevitable heat, the boys helped me dig two holes to hold the reclaimed signs. We mixed cement by hand

and set the newly painted signs in place, shoveling in the freshly mixed slop. We secured them with angular supports, and when the cement had cured two days later, we removed the supports and filled in the holes. The job was done. The new signs looked fabulous from our breezy balcony but would they make any difference or be completely ignored? Cars kept rushing through the intersection, some at breakneck speeds, and some slowing down ever so slightly. The accidents kept occurring, and I came to the inevitable age-old conclusion that you can't teach old dogs new tricks.

"Hey Dad," the boys asked, "Would you be willing to referee a basketball game between ACS and some kids from a neighborhood team?" I hesitated. I knew the style of basketball both sides played and I was wary of conflict on the American Cooperative School court. In the end I agreed but ended up paying a price for doing so. When the two teams assembled, my neighbor and I spelled out the rules for the match. I told the teams, in Dutch and in English, that there would be no foul language, and no excessive rough play. Violation of either rule would result in two points for the other team. I asked the teams if the rules were understood, and they all nodded their heads in agreement. And then the game began.

All went well as the score see-sawed back and forth for the first fifteen minutes. On a particular play, I heard a curse word that had been launched by a neighborhood team player. I awarded the ACS students two points and again warned the players that foul language would not be permitted. Nevertheless, it kept occurring and by the time the game was over, our missionary kids had defeated the neighborhood team. The other team was disgruntled over their loss, and I thought I had heard the last of it.

In the middle of the night I awoke to the sound of a car speeding down our cobblestone street, through the intersection with its freshly painted stop signs now in place, roaring past our home. As it did, I glanced to see someone hanging from the open car window and toss a projectile in the direction of our bedroom. A large stone came crashing through our bedroom window, shattering glass all over our bed and floor. The car sped off, raucous laughter emanating from the vehicle. I quickly got dressed, ran downstairs to our car parked underneath the house, upturned the ping pong table I had built for family fun, and set it up to protect the rear windshield, fearing that they would return with

171

more ammunition. My suspicions were confirmed as I heard the vehicle circle back through the neighborhood. This time two bodies were hanging out of the windows and as they passed by our house, larger stones were hurled right at the car. No further damage was caused as the ping pong table had done its job. The car zoomed past and as it did, two more objects were pitched at our neighbor, the one who had helped me referee the basketball game. The shattering of glass and subsequent flames confirmed that they had tossed two Molotov cocktails at his wooden gate, hoping to burn it down.

In the morning I called the police. As usual, I had to pick them up because they had no vehicle at their disposal. I was used to the routine by now so I drove over to the nearest police substation, took the policeman back to our house, and showed him the damage. I filed a complaint and drove the officer back to his post where he sat down and filled in a report, in triplicate, using carbon paper, on an old Remington manual typewriter. He asked me if I knew who had thrown the projectiles at our house. I told him I was quite sure. He said, "Mr. Speyers, if you can deliver a license plate number to this office, we'll apprehend the driver and take care of the matter." They were matter of fact but encouraging.

As I drove home, I had nagging doubts that the police would do anything. Normally, in the case of a traffic accident involving a foreigner, he is the first one considered to be at fault. It takes a lot of work, personal investigation, persistence, and evidence to overturn that type of thinking. A few years earlier, a colleague was standing perfectly still at a stop sign in his pickup truck, waiting for traffic to clear, when another vehicle plowed into him. John was unhurt. His door was severely damaged but the perpetrator came out of his car, claiming that John's car was slightly ahead of the faint marking on the roadway. The police agreed with the other driver and charged John, even though he was one of the most careful drivers I knew, and clearly not in the wrong.

As I weighed my options about the Molotov cocktails, I decided I would no longer pursue the incident, repair the damage myself and call it a day. I saw the vehicle frequently, circling through our neighborhood, but I chose to ignore it. That thinking saved us from many future difficult cultural situations.

Direct Attacks

In 1990, the unbelieving husband of a Christian Javanese woman attending Antoon's church was following him in his car. When Antoon noticed it, he stopped his car, ready to help him. The man walked up to his rolled down window, grabbed Antoon by the throat and squeezed so hard that he started to choke. The man kept saying, "I'm going to kill you! I'm going to kill you!" That's exactly what Antoon felt was going to happen. By God's grace, he let go and Antoon calmly said, "I'm going to the police!" Inexplicably, the man followed him in his own car to the nearest police station where he was arrested and spent ten uncomfortable days in a filthy jail cell. Clearly the Lord was protecting Antoon and was keeping him safe for His work. We sat in utter silence as Antoon told us his nightmare. Satan was at work to discourage and discredit the powerful, life-changing work of our national translator. More incidents followed.

In early April 1996 I walked over to the mailboxes inside our translation center. Peering inside, I let out a gasp. My heart sank because I noticed a letter from Antoon. I feared the worst. I hadn't seen our national translator for at least six weeks. Mailing a letter to me meant that something was not right. Normally, to contact me, he would call on the phone or stop by the office to chat. 80% of the Suriname Javanese New Testament was complete at the time. Only *Matthew* and *The Revelation* were left to translate. They were both large portions of Scripture but we were confident that with a final push, we could be done in 12-18 months.

I carefully opened the envelope, extracted the letter, my heart almost coming to a stop as I read the first line of his brief communication. "I quit," were the first two words. I was shocked but not totally surprised. The letter went on to explain why he was quitting the job of helping me with the translation of the Scriptures in the Suriname Javanese language. Since 1983 he had worked hard at understanding the mechanics of Bible translation. Something deeper, however, was driving him this time.

The letter stated that I should not try to contact him for several weeks. He needed time to think things through. Because of stress, he would be unable to continue translating the Scriptures for the 60,000 people who called themselves Suriname Javanese.

My tension rose trying to decipher the broader implications of the moment. If Antoon was going to quit as a translator, I would have to find someone else who could finish the job, but who? As a respected leader in his community, well-trained as a Bible translator and gifted with language, he was unmistakably the one God had put in our path. It dawned on me that the only tool at our disposal was prayer. I quickly composed a letter requesting urgent prayer for Antoon, and had several hundred copies printed which I mailed immediately to our partners, churches, and individuals alike.

About ten days went by. I couldn't stand the tension of not knowing what had made Antoon sick. I phoned him and heard his familiar voice on the other end. "Ed, I knew you couldn't wait. Let me be brief and explain what has happened to me. I can't work anymore because I'm exhausted. I'm spent. I have headaches and tire easily whenever I put pen to paper. I can't think when I want to translate. It's come to the point where I can't even carry on my normal duties as a pastor to my churches. To keep it brief, I want you to know that it's entirely your fault. You and Linda came to Suriname 17 years ago and first approached me about helping you with Bible translation. I listened and talked it over with Wanda, and we agreed that I should help you. You talked about how the churches would grow if we started to supply them with God's Word in their own language. I was skeptical at first but after a while, I knew that's what the Javanese needed. Now, many years later, we are on the verge of completing this important work and the churches are springing out of the ground like mushrooms. I'm frankly running around from one village to the next trying to keep up with the growth but my health is suffering as a result. So, I'm going to have to quit. I will finish this project but I don't know when. You should not look for another translator. Please be patient. I'll be back. In the meantime, I covet your prayers for a complete recovery."

I sat in stunned silence. The man the Lord has raised up to be our national translator had collapsed under the weight and burden of the work he had been called to do. He had suffered a major emotional, physical, social, and spiritual breakdown. And it was all my fault. I chuckled nervously at his choice of words. The triple load he was carrying had met its limits. Planting churches, administering those churches, and doing Bible translation would be a heavy burden for anyone to carry. We would just have to wait until his health improved.

But what was I supposed to do in the meantime? We couldn't leave the field and we couldn't move ahead without him. It was a Catch-22 situation. The Lord would have to prove Himself strong. On the other side of the coin we were blessed and reassured by the myriad number of heartfelt emails and letters from people who had responded positively to pray vigorously for Antoon's health. They promised to pray daily about this crisis. A spiritual tug-of-war was going on in heaven; it was just a question of who was going to win this battle. Our faith was being tested to the maximum.

We mustered as many prayer warriors together as possible and incessantly stormed the gates of heaven for both an answer to this latest challenge and for a complete recovery for Antoon's impaired health. Why did it seem like Satan always mounted his attacks when the finish line was in sight? Why did it feel like the evil one reared its ugly head whenever good things were being accomplished?

Many told and untold stories could fill the space here to underscore that we are in a spiritual battle when we deal with translating God's Word for the remaining people groups waiting for this precious resource. I asked myself, "Is Satan really that strong and does he somehow have a hand in trying to delay or destroy the works of God? Aren't we the ones who are called upon to destroy the works of the enemy instead? Isn't that made clear in 1 John 3:7-8? *Dear children, don't let anyone deceive you about this: When people do what is right, it shows that they are righteous, even as Christ is righteous. But when people keep on sinning, it shows that they belong to the devil, who has been sinning since the beginning. But the Son of God came to destroy the works of the devil.*"

Weeks morphed into months. Every time I called Antoon he told me I had to be patient. For months there seemed to be no improvement. "Ed," Antoon began, "every time I pick up my pen to translate, the headache and exhaustion returns. It's almost automatic. You'll just have to be patient. Believe me when I tell you that I will finish the translation, just not now." The frustration continued to mount.

The nagging thought of possibly having to find and train another translator was looking more and more inevitable. Was I just being impatient or was I trying to push Antoon into better health? At times I couldn't even sort out my own feelings about this conundrum.

More promises to pray daily about the situation arrived in our mailbox. In the end, we tallied fifty people who stood with us during this crisis. They would help carry the project through to completion but we didn't know that at the time. David and Mark were increasingly aware that we were under pressure as a family. We had envisioned being done with the translation work when David would graduate from high school so we could leave together as a family. It appeared unlikely that it would happen within that time frame.

Just before leaving on our furlough I visited Antoon one last time. He was still struggling with his health but minor improvements could be seen. Were we on the edge of a breakthrough?

We traveled throughout North America, gathering more prayer support along the many miles. Every now and then, I would receive a communiqué from Antoon about his improving health. There seemed to be a crack appearing in Satan's defense. The more we traveled and the more we gathered together our prayer forces, the wider the crack became. Our faith was being tested but it was holding strong. More people signed up to see the project through to its completion.

When we returned to Suriname for what would be our final term, we were met by a man I hardly recognized. Antoon appeared robust and healthy, ready to work. When he put his pen to paper, he did so with authority and confidence. On a weekly basis he showed up with newly translated chapters of *The Revelation*. It was all I could do to keep up with keyboarding the material. He was giving everything to me, handwritten in pencil, on reams of paper, like he had always done. We raced through *The Revelation* and dove into *Matthew's Gospel*. As we motored on, I was reminded about the tobacco fields of southern Ontario I worked in as a teenager. The farmer told me that the 'horse had smelled the barn', when he broke free from his chain pulling the full boat of freshly picked tobacco. Had Antoon 'smelled the barn', with the finish line in sight?

The calendar turned to 1999 as we watched the miracle unfold. We called in our international translation consultant to check the quality of the New Testament bookends. The consultant had previously checked a number of our other New Testament books but this time she said that the quality was superior to anything else Antoon had translated.

When he put the final words in place to the 8,000-verse document known as the New Testament, we organized a lavish celebration at the translation center to thank God for His faithfulness and steadfastness. In typical Javanese fashion, we dressed up in our Indonesian finery, ordered a large sheet cake, and the Suriname Branch celebrated with us. A short program was put together. I asked Antoon to sit at a table covered with grass mats and Indonesian cultural items. He put his pencil to paper and 'translated' the final words of Matthew 28. '*And teach them to obey everything I have commanded you. And I will be with you always, to the end of the age.*' The translation was done. Proofreading, typesetting, checking, re-checking, and layout, all lay before us but the big job we had come to do was finished at last. Exhilaration coursed through my veins. The final steps of the entire process were just around the corner.

BURN YOUR BED

The 500th

In February 1999, four months before we left Suriname for the last time, I flew to Dallas to prepare our New Testament for typesetting and final editing. I was warned the process would take no less than two months. Several translators from other countries were there with their treasured manuscripts. Earlier, the Printing Arts Department had sent a long list of requirements needing to be fulfilled before showing up on their doorstep. I had meticulously followed each step and was confident it would not take two months, but prepared if it did.

In 1995 Wycliffe published the 400th New Testament completed by the organization and the 500th would be announced soon. A committee had to decide which language represented the new milestone. When is a translation finally complete? When it has been drafted? When it's gone through its final checks? When the editing is done? When it goes to the printers? When it's published? As the committee deliberated, I too, wondered when the announcement would be made. During the final edit, I asked those assisting me. They said a translation in Africa was being considered. The gentleman laughed, "Your translation doesn't qualify."

"Oh, I understand," I replied, "it was more out of curiosity than anything else." Deep inside I heard a quiet voice say, "Wouldn't it just be like God to give you, the former 'zero', the honor of being the 500th?"

The hours sped by quickly. Within a week we were 90% complete with the typesetting when we hit a big snag. Almost twenty percent of the book of *The Revelation* was missing from the digital manuscript. I had made several backup copies in case of an error but when we checked those, we discovered that the error had been replicated there too. I was starting to have visions of Antoon being called to the office to re-translate the last few chapters of The Book. I was about to panic so made a phone call to the Suriname office. We discovered that the software program we used had a glitch in it. The original document was safe and secure on my computer in South America. With a sigh of relief, I settled back into the checking routine and within a few hours, the correct edition of *The Revelation* arrived by email.

My spirit was soaring when the last jot and tittle were in place. The process had taken only eight working days, a record-setting milestone for this department that assisted translators in preparing their priceless manuscripts for printing and publication. An announcement was made over the intercom system that the Suriname Javanese New Testament was ready for publication and would be sent off to Korea for printing. We celebrated with cake and ice cream, giving thanks to God for his unfailing care and protection. I said good-bye to my colleagues Glenn and Sarah who had graciously housed me for those days and flew back to Suriname earlier than expected, much to the great delight of the entire family.

The accumulation of 20 years of goods needed to be taken care of. Together, Linda and I decided that the only items we would take back from Suriname would include her sewing machine, my heavy tools, wedding silverware, and the boys' Legos. It could all fit, quite easily, into one homemade crate that would sit on the back of a pickup truck. We pared our lifestyle down to a box that measured 4 feet by 4 feet by 8 feet. It was both frightening and liberating. How does one lift such a big heavy box?

I remembered that the Chinese supermarket down the road had a small forklift. The proprietor, who knew us well from our many shopping trips, personally came over with his machinery and lifted the wooden box with ease onto the back of a waiting flatbed truck. A shake of the hand took care of the details. There were so many ways that we had grown to love this country. Making friendships had been a delight. Getting to know our neighbors was wonderful. Some things were enacted with such ease that we frequently still long for those experiences. But, we also experienced the frustrations of needless delays and an overabundance of paperwork. We have concluded over the years that no place is perfect, far from it. Each place has its advantages and disadvantages. The secret is to be content wherever life brings you and make friends, lots of them.

Then came the most wonderful surprise ever, in an email message.

"Edward and Linda, after doing some thorough and careful research, the Wycliffe Bible Translators has made the decision to announce the completion of the 500th New Testament translation. The committee has chosen the Suriname Javanese New Testament translation as the final candidate for this esteemed honor. Do you accept this challenge?"

I stared at the email in disbelief and once again read those incredible words. I ran downstairs to my colleagues who were on coffee break. When I announced the news, they all clapped and shouted with overwhelming joy. It was June 1, 1999. In just three days we would be leaving Suriname for good. We were scheduled to return once the New Testament had been printed and shipped from Korea and a tentative date for the dedication of the 500th New Testament was set for March 2000. God had the last word in this discussion.

BURN YOUR BED

The Dedication

I was peering into the inky sky, straining my eyes, hoping for at least a glimpse of the landing lights of the Beechcraft King Air 200 but there were none. Surely they can't be that far away now, I thought. Suddenly, two small pinpricks appeared over the darkening western horizon. As they grew brighter and brighter, I felt my excitement grow. Could that really be them or was it another passenger jet making its way to Zanderij, Suriname's international airport? No, the lights were too close together for an airliner.

As the aircraft made its approach, I could almost hear the chatter between the tower and the pilot. Here they were, on final. The 10-seat twin turboprop touched down on the 10,000' runway, as we had done countless times over the twenty years that we lived in Suriname. Tears started to well up as I watched the aircraft taxi to a parking spot on the tarmac. I observed the plane disgorge its ten passengers and had to restrain myself from running out onto the field to greet my new friends.

The day before, the pilot and his passengers had left North Carolina to help us celebrate the dedication of our New Testament. They had stopped overnight in the Caribbean and completed the two day journey to join us for the festivities. And now here they were, on the ground. Forty more invited guests had flown on Surinam Airway's only commercial jet from Miami, landed at Zanderij and settled into their hotel rooms in Paramaribo. Today's arrivals completed the list of fifty people invited from the United States and Canada to join us for the celebration of the completion and dedication of the 500th New Testament.

Was it really possible after twenty years of living in this tropical jungle, that the job was finally complete? Hundreds of dedications had taken place before ours in dozens of countries, each one special. SIL's Suriname Branch leadership had worried that the dedication ceremony might be too small but I reassured them that the Suriname Javanese were accomplished aficionados in organizing these types of events. Linda and I had observed them for two decades and I reassured the executive committee there was no reason for concern. If anybody knew how to throw a big party, it would be the Javanese.

My mind floated back to our days in the village when we experienced some of those large celebrations. Eleven-year-old boys cowered in fear as the day of their circumcision loomed close. The village elders made a big deal of this rite of passage, and the occasion was always replete with plenty of partying and drinking, celebrating this important milestone in a boy's life and transition to manhood. There wasn't a soul in the entire village that didn't know of a boy's greatest dread. I can still see David, as a one-year-old, outside of our little village home, playing with an old bucket filled with water. His cloth diaper, now soaked by the spilling water, had settled down around his ankles. Young village boys stared in disbelief and jealousy, realizing that their painful ordeal was still lying ahead of them. The news spread like wildfire that David was 'wis sunat'.

Marriage celebrations likewise, were colorful and full of Asian tradition. When a 15-year-old neighbor girl announced that she was pregnant, she was sent to the mosque to talk to the village priests, and her marriage was hastily arranged. She and her 16-year-old boyfriend were told by the priests that if the marriage didn't work out, they should return to the mosque and the priests would annul the nuptial. The celebration, however, was over the top and the village gathered together with grand festivities lasting well into the night, in support of the young couple. Yes, the Javanese of Suriname knew how to throw a party.

Another festival, Kleting Kuning, or, The Yellow Princess, usually started at 11 P.M. and lasted throughout the night. By the time midnight rolled around, Linda and I would excuse ourselves and head for home, too tired to keep our drooping eyelids open. The hours between midnight and sunup are the coolest hours of the day. Why not party when the conditions are right?

Our biggest challenge was trying to stay awake into the wee hours of the morning. There was never a lack of food at these occasions, much of which had multiple, unknown ingredients. We sampled everything and politely turned down what didn't agree with our palate, which wasn't much. All of the food was made from scratch, village ladies working together well in advance to prepare snacks, pluck chickens, and stir fry hot spicy condiments in a wok over an open outdoor fire. Crispy fried banana and cassava chips were stored in large black trash bags and empty 5-gallon buckets. It was a community affair with the women cooking and the men setting up temporary shelters with galvanized sheeting and electric lights.

When the branch leadership expressed concern about the Javanese needing some assistance in organizing the celebration of the dedication for the New Testament, we knew they needn't have worried. As we gathered in the large hall on that Saturday evening, March 18, 2000, Linda and I looked around at the mass of people that had gathered there. We were both shocked and thankful. We had never seen so many Javanese people in one place at one time. Our guests from the US and Canada occupied a portion near the front. Also in attendance in the front rows were the Minister of Education, the American ambassador, Surinamese pastors and other government dignitaries. The hall held 1,000 people and every seat was taken. A video crew had been sent down by Wycliffe and spent four full days filming the historic events.

As the dedication ceremony started, Linda and I found ourselves along with Antoon and his wife, Wanda, on the front row, as the guests of honor. My mind drifted back to my growing up days and my father's discouraging words. My high school teacher's disappointing remarks reverberated in my mind. If only they could see this now, I thought. As the festivities played out, Antoon couldn't contain himself. Time after time, he turned to me to comment on something that was taking place this special evening. But there was one comment that sticks out in my mind more than any other. "Ed," he said, "your work in Suriname is done but mine is just beginning." I quietly thought, "Yes, Lord, he gets it." It would be his job to train up leaders and elders in scripturally and culturally appropriate ways. Planting and feeding local churches was now possible. Antoon's attempt to plant churches in the early years had met with mixed results. He concluded some years into the translation process that God's Word needs to be available in the mother tongue if local churches are going to survive and thrive. Those churches would raise up leaders and never become dependent on foreign guidance or resources to grow and multiply.

Years earlier, when the translation was well under way and the Javanese were starting to turn to the Lord, Antoon asked me if I would serve on his board of elders. I politely refused. "Antoon," I said, "much of the New Testament has already been translated. Many of your people can now read. I was trained as a Bible translator, not as a church leader. Search the Scriptures, and along with your best people, determine what the Lord would have you do. You don't want your churches looking like they've mimicked some western model." He fully agreed and began to train elders and leaders. It was satisfying to see him take the lead and demonstrate that a first century church movement could grow up amongst the Javanese. At the dedication, that proof was clearly visible. The Javanese church had exploded in growth from one miniscule village church of just ten people (Dessa) to more than a dozen churches planted across the northern coast of this piece of tropical real estate, serving hundreds of believers. In the 1990s, the Suriname Javanese church was the fastest growing church in the entire region.

The highlight of the evening's celebration focused on the beautifully choreographed dance routine performed by a dozen Javanese dancers to the traditional melody of gamelans and drums. This was a first to have a gamelan orchestra ensemble at a Christian celebration. The dance followed the progression of the sixteen long years it took to complete the translation of the New Testament. The final dance depicted brightly clothed angels dancing, holding the Word of God. At first they held up the Dutch Scriptures but there was no response from the angel dancers. Then the translation of the New Testament in Suriname Javanese commenced and the angels clearly depicted this part of the dance by handing out portions as they were translated. But as the Javanese community came into a relationship with the Messiah Jesus Christ, problems and challenges starting to rear their ugly heads.

A dark, Satan figure with a grotesque mask and long dreadlocks appeared on the stage, threatening to undo or harm the work that the Holy Spirit had begun under these displaced Asian peoples. Now the angels banded together. They mounted their attack and began a barrage of assaults on Satan, much to the delight and applause of the now fully engaged crowd. But Satan was not to be fooled and redoubled his own attacks. They sparred back and forth several times. The crowd seemed unsure who was going to win this battle. Antoon leaned over and through his tears he said, "Ed, do you remember all of the opposition we faced over these last few years?" I nodded in full agreement, remembering the untold attacks we had encountered over the years, especially those that came towards the end of the translation process.

My mind reeled as I thought about the village encounters, beginning with the arduous task of collecting language data twenty years earlier, the chicken man, the graveyard experiences, the many times we couldn't understand what was being said, my hand injury, the loss of my language helper back in Dessa, the military coups and counter-coups that seemed determined to move the entire process across the Atlantic to the Netherlands, the thrown rocks, and the Molotov cocktails.

By now the angels had gathered their collective strength. Slowly and methodically they mounted one last effort to dispel Satan from their midst. Just then, a man in bright white clothing appeared. The crowd, now fully into it, recognized him as Jesus. He came to Satan, grabbed both flailing arms and deftly put them behind his back, immobilizing the evil one. The angels joined him and succeeded in kicking the foreboding Satan figure off the stage, much to the relief and growing applause of the enthralled crowd. I glanced at Antoon. His mind had been working as hard as mine. Our fifty guests from the US and Canada hadn't missed a beat of this thrilling performance. No words were needed to convey the intended message.

As the time for the presentation of the newly translated Suriname Javanese New Testament arrived, Antoon, Wanda, Linda and I were invited to the stage. I briefly spoke from the podium, telling the crowd that Suriname had become a richer country that evening in March 2000. Antoon also made a short speech. As we prepared to leave the stage, something happened that shocked me; he reached over and gave me a short but firm hug. In the twenty years I had known him, we had never touched one another except for frequent handshakes. I was floored by this kind gesture and treasure it as one of the finest moments of our years in Suriname.

As the evening's thrilling presentation concluded, a strange thought struck me. I was 50 years old. This was the 500th New Testament celebration with Wycliffe involvement, and it all happened to a scared young boy who had been called a big zero. The Lord had taken me from 0 to 500 in 50!

Linda, Ed, and Antoon, at the presentation
of the Suriname Javanese New Testament.

Epilogue

In 1999 we came back to a completely different culture than what we left in 1979. Shortly after landing at Miami's International airport, we found ourselves at the grocery store checkout counter. The cashier asked, "Paper or plastic?" What a strange request, I thought. I turned to Linda who had a puzzled look on her face and shrugged her shoulders. It must mean that she's asking us how we want to pay for our purchases so I said, "I'll pay cash." In Suriname we were never asked these strange questions.

It took us three or four years before we felt like we had our feet on the ground again. Reverse culture shock is difficult; at times painful and embarrassing.

David started college immediately and Mark entered the 10th grade, a difficult transitionary period. They both went from a classroom of 25 students, grades 9-12 at ACS, to schools in Michigan with 1,000 students. We all had long and difficult rows to hoe.

The boys are married now. Mark is married to Fernanda and they live in the concrete jungle of Toronto. They both work for high tech firms in Canada's largest city. David is married to Lisa and returned to the jungles of South America. They have two daughters. David serves as a missionary pilot, flying a float plane in Peru over the tributaries of the Amazon.

My mother was well taken care of by my sister and her husband for over 25 years until she died in 2007 at the advanced age of 94.

Linda and I live in Tennessee working as Wycliffe recruiters throughout the South looking for the next generation of Bible translators.

The Suriname Javanese New Testament, the 500th New Testament completed by the Wycliffe Bible Translators, shown with the dust cover.